1991

# A New Iraq?

# THE WASHINGTON PAPERS

. . . intended to meet the need for an authoritative, yet prompt, public appraisal of the major developments in world affairs.

**President, CSIS:** David M. Abshire

**Series Editor:** Walter Laqueur

**Director of Publications:** Nancy B. Eddy

**Managing Editor:** Donna R. Spitler

## MANUSCRIPT SUBMISSION

*The Washington Papers* and Praeger Publishers welcome inquiries concerning manuscript submissions. Please include with your inquiry a curriculum vitae, synopsis, table of contents, and estimated manuscript length. Manuscripts must be between 120–200 double-spaced typed pages. All submissions will be peer reviewed. Submissions to *The Washington Papers* should be sent to *The Washington Papers*; The Center for Strategic and International Studies; 1800 K Street NW; Suite 400; Washington, DC 20006. Book proposals should be sent to Praeger Publishers; One Madison Avenue; New York NY 10010.

The Washington Papers/133

# A New Iraq?

## The Gulf War and Implications for U.S. Policy

### Frederick W. Axelgard

Published with The Center for
Strategic and International Studies
Washington, D.C.

PRAEGER

New York
Westport, Connecticut
London

**Library of Congress Cataloging-in-Publication Data**

Axelgard, Frederick W.
  A New Iraq?

  (The Washington Papers, ISSN 0278-937X ; 133)
  "Published with the Center for Strategic and
International Studies, Washington, D.C."
  Includes index.
  1. Iraq – Politics and government.  2. Iraqi-Iranian
Conflict, 1980 –      – Influence.  I. Title.  II. Series.
DS79.65.A94   1988   955′.054        88-2403
ISBN 0-275-93013-0 (alk. paper)
ISBN 0-275-93014-9 (pbk.: alk. paper)

Library of Congress Catalog Card Number: 88-2403
ISBN: 0-275-93013-0 (cloth)
        0-275-93014-9 (paper)

First published in 1988

Praeger Publishers, One Madison Avenue, New York, NY 10010
A division of Greenwood Press, Inc.

Printed in the United States of America

The paper used in this book complies with the Permanent
Paper Standard issued by the National Information Standards
Organization (Z39.48-1984).

10  9  8  7  6  5  4  3  2  1

# Contents

v

# Foreword

To what extent should the United States forge a close relationship with President Saddam Hussein's Ba'thi government? Some see that regime, whatever its current public posture, as congenitally hostile to U.S. aims in the Middle East. Others contend that it has mellowed and that a sufficient mutuality of interests now exists between the two countries to ensure longer-term cooperation. In devising policy toward Iraq, U.S. administrations must weigh such differing attitudes. These differences reflect congressional and public disquiet and rise from diffuse, but interrelated, elements.

First, until the Iran-Iraq war began in 1980 and even afterward, Iraq was little known to other than a limited number of official Americans and academic specialists. To the extent most members of Congress or the U.S. public thought of Iraq, it was generally in negative terms. After all, Iraq had consistently opposed U.S. efforts to achieve an Arab-Israeli peace. For years the Ba'thi leadership of Iraq had challenged the pervasive U.S. presence in the Middle East. Israel, whose influence on U.S. thinking about the Middle East is considerable, viewed Iraq as a mortal enemy. In 1981 it bombed Iraq's Osirak reactor, claiming the reactor was intended to provide Iraq with a nuclear military capability. Many Americans believed this charge. Still worse, Iraq had provided hospitality and support for Abu Nidal–directed Palestinian terrorists, a cardinal sin in U.S. eyes that was not to be simply effaced by Baghdad's eventual expulsion of the group.

Second, until the late 1970s, moderate Arab friends of the United States – Egypt, Saudi Arabia, Jordan, and others – had serious reservations about Iraq's Ba'thi leadership. During Anwar Sadat's period, Egypt rightly saw Baghdad as determined to subvert his efforts to achieve peace with Israel. After Camp David and the Egyptian-Israeli peace treaty, Saddam Hussein spearheaded the Arab effort to penalize and ostracize Egypt. On another level, the regimes of Saudi Arabia and Jordan suspected that the Iraqi leadership sought the overthrow of monarchical systems in those countries. Kuwait, although hardly close to the United States, was recurrently threatened by Iraqi designs on all or part of its territory. In the 1970s, Iraq had provided arms for the Dhofari insurgency against the sultan of Oman. Baghdad seemed to conduct policies in the Arab world that consciously ran counter to U.S. interests and were patently hegemonial in objective.

Third, some questioned Iraq's internal political stability. With Iraq's sizable and restive Shi'a majority and its recurrent Kurdish problem in the north, informed U.S. analysts speculated that unresolved ethnic and Islamic sectarian fissures in Iraq's demographic structure would sooner or later unravel the sociopolitical fabric of the state. The Ba'thi leadership's recourse to military action against the Kurds, coupled with sometimes brutal actions against suspected Shi'a dissenters, were viscerally deplored by Americans as inconsistent with universal human rights concepts. The regime, seen by Americans as relying perforce on police measures in order to remain in office, could hardly endear itself to a democratically oriented society or, on another level, offer promise of long-range domestic tranquillity.

Fourth, since the overthrow of the monarchy in July 1958, successive Iraqi republican regimes had assiduously allied themselves with the Soviet Union. Soviet military equipment was supplied to Iraq, and Soviet technical advisers abounded in that country. Although Baghdad denied accepting Soviet political tutelage, a widespread U.S. impression existed that Iraq had become a Soviet client state. Because U.S. policy had long sought to exclude the Soviets from the strategically important Persian–Arabian Gulf area, Iraq seemed consciously to pursue policies that provided the Soviet Union with a political and, to some extent at least, a military lodgment in the Gulf. For U.S. policymakers and Americans in general, this was onerous and censorious.

Fifth, in considering the respective strategic positions of Iraq and Iran, the United States had consistently viewed Iran as more important real estate. During the shah's period, Iran was regarded as a U.S. ally; conversely, Iraq was seen as a Soviet-influenced opponent. Moreover, the disparity in strength between Iran and Iraq gave the shah's Iran the edge in U.S. geopolitical thinking. Even the advent of the Iranian Islamic Republic in 1979 did not initially alter this U.S.-perceived strategic equation. For a time the hope existed, until the humiliating hostage crisis, that somehow the United States could still retain a viable relationship with Iran because of the latter's contiguous border with the Soviet Union and its shared perceptions of a Soviet threat. Although illusory, this attitude meant Iraq remained ignored and relegated to a political dustbin. In fairness, this was not only a function of U.S. myopia; Iraq, through its own policies, shared in shaping negative U.S. attitudes toward it.

Sixth, Iraq had broken diplomatic relations with the United States in 1967. For years, Washington's occasional efforts to restore these relations with Iraq were rebuffed by the Ba'thi regime. A U.S. Interests Section existed in Baghdad, but diplomatic dialogue was usually limited to lower-level Foreign Ministry officials. Not until 1984, by which time the Iran-Iraq war had been under way for four years, did Baghdad act to reestablish diplomatic relations with the United States. Many Americans, both official and private, saw this belated Iraqi initiative as a tactical expedient, prompted by desperation following Iranian military successes in driving Iraqi forces back across the border. Had the "Lion of Babylon," as Saddam Hussein allegorizes the state, permanently muffled its roar? Or would the Iraqi regime revert to earlier anti-American attitudes once the war was over? There were many Americans (and Israelis) who believed it would do precisely that. True, Egypt and especially King Hussein of Jordan insist the Iraqi leadership has undergone an irrevocable change of heart and no longer opposes further Arab-Israeli peace negotiations. Perhaps so, but who can be sure? For the first Iraqi ambassador to return to Washington, Nizar Hamdoon, persuading Americans of Iraq's sincerity was an uphill effort and, to a considerable extent, remains thus for his successor.

Seventh, notwithstanding the equivocation of UN Resolution 598 of July 20, 1987 on responsibility for the conflict, many Americans believe Iraq began the war. To the extent they recall the events of 1980, they think of the November 28 Iraqi armed invasion of Iranian territory as aggression. Iraq's contention that the war began several weeks earlier with Iranian-incited assassination attempts against Iraqi leaders is viewed with skepticism. Mutual Iraqi and Iranian subversive acts against one another in the months before the Iraqi military invasion are dismissed by many Americans as comparable, reciprocal harassment by both sides and hardly justification for armed invasion of Iranian territory. In the spate of charges and countercharges, many Americans find it hard to judge, or to care, which came first – the Iraqi chicken or the Iranian egg.

That Baghdad should today find itself hard-pressed by Iranian manpower superiority, one body of U.S. opinion strongly argues, is retribution for the short-sighted Iraqi resort to force. Moreover, many Americans who are concerned about the current massing of U.S. naval power in the Gulf and want early disengagement from the area blame Iraq for ignoring Washington's urgings to cease attacks on Iranian oil installations and shuttle tankers and thus for prolonging the conflict with attendant personnel risks and costs to U.S. naval forces in the Gulf. They may acknowledge Iraqi acceptance of UN Resolution 598, but see as arcane the dispute about sequential or inverse implementation of its provisions. Nor, of course, did the May 17, 1987 Iraqi attack on the U.S.S. *Stark* and the resultant loss of 37 U.S. lives – though inadvertent – enhance Iraq's image in this country.

Even as debate on the above persists, however, the United States is beginning to realize that Iran must not be permitted to defeat Iraq. Until perhaps a year or so ago, most U.S. officials and pundits complacently believed that neither Iraq nor Iran could achieve a decisive victory. Both would eventually exhaust themselves, be forced to conclude peace, and thus have their potential mischief-making capabilities in the Gulf hamstrung for the foreseeable future. Since the Iranian military successes, first in the Fao peninsula in 1986 and then in the Fish Lake area of southern Iraq in 1987, a gradual change in U.S. thinking has occurred. A growing number of Americans now suggest the possibility of an Iranian victory. It is dawning on Americans (and on some Israelis) that a decisive Iranian Islamic fundamentalist military success could be disastrous, not only for the friendly Arab polities of the oil-rich Gulf area but for the Middle East as a whole. The deployment of U.S. naval units to the Gulf area cannot appreciably affect the outcome of the land conflict. Despite Iran's straitened economy, Tehran has the manpower and seemingly the motivation to conduct a prolonged war of attrition against Iraq; for its part, Iraq may not be able to sustain such a conflict indefinitely. Peace needs to be restored to the Gulf area as expeditiously as possible. As concern about Iran increases, Iraq thus benefits – not because of anything it has done to redeem its image, but because of new U.S. perceptions of a graver, more imminent threat to its interests.

In truth, Iraq has in the past four decades undergone a bemusing series of political metamorphoses. In the immediate post–World War II period, the then Iraqi monarchical regime was closely allied with Britain and was an active proponent of Arab unity schemes, such as Prime Minister Nuri Said's Union of the Fertile Crescent. In 1955, it was a founding member of the Baghdad Pact, a U.S.-conceived "northern tier" security alignment aimed at containing a putative Soviet thrust toward the Gulf. As a result, U.S. military assistance was provided to Iraq for a number of years. The sanguinary overthrow of the Hashemite monarchy in July 1958, through a military *putsch*, spawned an Iraqi republic, politically anti-Western and with considerable domestic communist influence. An almost dreary series of military regimes ensued, usually through coups, until the establishment in 1964 of a pan-Arab, secularist, socialist Ba'thi government. On the one hand, that regime's articulated policies were strongly anti-American; on the other, it challenged Egyptian leadership aspirations in the Arab world.

With Iraq's withdrawal from the Baghdad Pact in 1959, its relations with Iran had steadily deteriorated over issues such as the Shatt al-Arab boundary dispute and the Kurdish problem. An Algerian-brokered agreement between Iraq and Iran in 1975 appeared to assuage tensions between the two neighboring states and included a mechanism for resolving differences that might arise between them. That agreement was denounced by Saddam Hussein in 1980, following the advent of the Iranian Islamic Republic, when Iraq forcibly reclaimed its previous boundary. At the time, many believed that Saddam Hussein was deliberately seeking to capitalize on the chaotic internal situation in Iran and, in the process, to project Iraq as the premier champion and protector of Arab interests in the Gulf area.

The Arab states of the Gulf could empathize with Iraq's anti-Iranian stance, but such sympathy was coupled with deep concern about what a victorious Ba'thi-dominated Iraq might mean for the Gulf area. The Iranian success in repulsing the Iraqi attack and in eventually occupying parts of southern Iraq altered their political calculus. Now

Iraq became the boundary of defense for the Arab side of the Gulf and received from Kuwait and Saudi Arabia, in particular, generous financial support and access to transit facilities. Slowly the Iraqi Ba'thi government's political attitudes also seemed to change, as it probed for improved relations with the United States it had previously rebuffed.

Fred Axelgard's study offers valuable perspectives on the complexities of past and present Iraqi politics. His is an advocacy brief that pleads for a more positive U.S. policy toward Iraq. Although offering a balanced assessment of the Iraqi regime and past and present U.S. policy toward it, he accentuates the positive. His thesis is cogent and clear.

Even before the outbreak of the Iran-Iraq war, subtle signals of Baghdad's desire for better relations with the United States could be detected. Despite the absence of diplomatic relations and the often strident Iraqi political challenge to the U.S. position in the Gulf, Iraq had shown a marked interest in U.S. technology and goods and services during the 1970s. This interest, Axelgard suggests, was intended to pave the way for eventual improved political dialogue. Equally important, beginning in 1984, were indications of a recognition by the Ba'thi regime in Baghdad that Israel was a permanent factor in the Middle East and that Iraq would be prepared to accept any settlement as long as the latter was agreeable to the Palestinians. Similarly, Iraq's relations with Egypt, Jordan, and the Arab states of the Gulf have substantially improved, despite occasional rhetoric by Baghdad's leaders charging inadequate Arab financial support.

On the home front, while brutally coercive in his grip on the Iraqi government, Saddam Hussein has succeeded in establishing himself as the indisputable leader of the state—the "struggler leader," as he has come to be known since the outbreak of the war. He has "Ba'thized" the Iraqi officer corps, whatever that means, and has created a sense of national cohesion among the Iraqi people, except for the Kurds. Through cooperation with Turkey, nevertheless, the Kurdish threat can be contained. Communist members of the erstwhile National Front have been eliminated. The long-standing restiveness of Iraqi Shi'is is controlled by a carrot-and-stick approach. Apart from a few instances, the Ayatollah Khomeini's appeals to fellow Shi'a sectarians in Iraq have fallen on deaf ears. Arab ethnicity seems more powerful than sectarian affinity. Moreover, despite the exigencies of war, Iraq has been able to export petroleum, largely through Turkey and Saudi Arabia, which gives it a continuing strong economic base. All things considered, Saddam Hussein's regime should be able to endure, even though it cannot win the conflict.

The United States, Axelgard opines, has for too long been locked into a policy of indifference toward Iraq. Such an attitude is outdated. Whether one likes it or not, Iraq will remain a major factor affecting Gulf and Middle East politics. If the United States conducts itself properly, prospects are good that a postwar Iraqi regime will pursue policies at least generally compatible with maintaining U.S. interests in the Middle East. More positive U.S. support for Iraq is needed. In the immediate future, as long as the war continues, the United States should do all it can to ensure Iraq's survival. Because arms cannot be provided in the face of likely congressional objections, U.S. agricultural aid and intelligence information should continue to be extended. In the postwar era, U.S. relations with Iraq should be broadened through political and commercial contacts.

Axelgard's thesis is provocative and well argued. Whatever cooperation currently exists between Washington and Baghdad, a legacy of mutual suspicion lingers. U.S. perfidy in covertly providing arms to Iran—though now stopped, it is hoped—must clearly concern the Iraqi regime, whatever its public posture. Axelgard is a positivist, and a certain amount of faith is needed to accept his prognostication of likely future Iraqi policies. Many Americans still suspect that any improvements in Iraq's attitude toward the United States or, say, toward Israel or a Middle East peace process are a postural response to its need for outside support in its current difficult situation. Nevertheless, the possibility that a postwar Iraq, under Ba'th Party leadership, will conduct itself more cooperatively with the United States on the Middle East political scene than was the case in the past surely deserves a fair test. The alternative—an Iranian Islamic fundamentalist success—is too fraught with area-wide dangers to contemplate with equanimity.

Axelgard's book is an incisive analysis of the strengths and weaknesses of the current Iraqi regime and, equally so, the vacillation of U.S. policy toward Iraq over the years. It offers U.S. policymakers and analysts sound insights for a more constructive approach to the current leadership of that venerable, but perennially roiled, "land of the twin rivers."

Hermann Frederick Eilts
Director of the Center for International Relations
Boston University
and former U.S. Ambassador to
Saudi Arabia and Egypt

# About the Author

Frederick W. Axelgard is a research fellow in Middle East Studies at the Center for Strategic and International Studies. His focus is the Iran-Iraq war, the political and economic development of the Arab countries of the Persian Gulf, and U.S. policy toward the Gulf. His writings have appeared in *Current History*, the *Washington Post*, the *Christian Science Monitor*, the *Los Angeles Times*, the *Chicago Tribune*, and numerous other papers and journals. He is the editor of *Iraq in Transition* (Westview, 1986) and the author of *U.S.-Arab Relations: The Iraq Dimension* (The National Council on U.S.-Arab Relations, 1985), as well as of a forthcoming study on U.S. policy toward Iraq from 1945 to 1958. He was educated at Brigham Young University (B.A.) and the Fletcher School of Law and Diplomacy (M.A.L.D.).

# A New Iraq?

# 1

# Iraq: The Gulf War and the Struggle for Legitimacy

How has the Iran-Iraq war affected the long-term political development of Iraq? This question—the central concern of this study—has seldom been emphasized in the vast and expanding literature analyzing the war. Analysis of the war, if it addresses Iraqi politics at all, has focused on whether the regime of Saddam Hussein can survive this Iranian offensive, that morale crisis, or yet another encounter with nervous foreign creditors. It has therefore seemed sufficient to observe that while Iraq is being severely tested at its sectarian, ethnic, and ideological seams, the country is holding on—for the time being.

But preoccupation with "the time being" overlooks the fact that the enduring and painful war with Iran has probably become the most important political event in Iraq's modern history. An analytical step back from the day-to-day hellishness of the conflict brings into focus several significant milestones that reflect important changes in Iraq's internal structure and its international position:

- "Revolutionary" regimes have now governed in Iraq for a longer time than did the Hashemite monarchy, which ruled from Iraq's independence in 1932 until the revolution of 1958.

- The present Ba'thi government has held power in Iraq for nearly two decades, thereby stabilizing what has historically been one of the Middle East's most infirm political systems.
- The war has helped reorient Iraq's military away from its traditional role as the arbiter of domestic politics by forcing it to focus on the defense of Iraq against external threats.
- Iraq's growing network of oil pipelines is giving this almost landlocked country more economic security than it has had since becoming a major oil exporter more than four decades ago.
- By containing the expansion of Iran's Islamic revolution, Iraq has played a major role in regional defense for the first time since the 1950s and the Baghdad Pact.
- Because of sustained international attention to the war, Iraq is now acknowledged as a power to reckon with in the Persian Gulf; this status has long been an objective of the Ba'thi regime.
- Its wartime regional alliances confirm that Iraq has abandoned the radical "rejectionist" camp and broken sharply with its long-standing image as the "odd man out" in Arab politics.
- Finally, Iraq has progressed toward a potent, balanced relationship with the superpowers, with both the Soviet Union and the United States providing important support for Iraq's position in the war.

These observations suggest that more than seven years into the war with Iran, Iraq has more to win than just military survival. Also at stake is the potential transformation of Iraq's political culture. For 65 years Iraq has struggled inconclusively to become a viable nation-state, and the protracted war has put unprecedented pressure on Iraq to justify its existence to its regional neighbors, to the world at large, and most important, to its own people. If it successfully survives the conflict with Iran, Iraq will also realize a major achievement in its quest for a coherent national identity, regional coexistence, and international acceptability – the trappings of a modern nation-state that have so long eluded Iraq.

## The Struggle for Political Viability, 1932–1975

This study has two basic purposes: first, to suggest that the war has changed Iraq's internal politics as well as its relations with the outside world; and second, to urge that these changes justify a serious rethinking of U.S. policy toward Iraq, both in the near term and in the context of addressing U.S. interests in the Gulf after Khomeini's demise. To set the stage for the chapters that follow, these two topics – political change in Iraq and U.S. policy toward Iraq – should be put in perspective.

The political history of modern Iraq has been troubled, to say the least. The country has had little success in either maintaining a stable political climate at home or presenting a consistent, responsible image regionally and internationally. The title of this chapter refers to the problematic nature of Iraq's historic struggle to develop legitimate governance at home and fulfill a serious role in the regional and global scheme of things. Many authoritative volumes have been written on the fitful emergence of this comparatively new and relatively small country.[1] For our purposes here, however, it must suffice to identify and briefly elaborate on some of the enduring themes from Iraq's modern political history.

### Political Instability and Military Intervention

The decades since Iraq's creation from pieces of the Ottoman Empire in 1920 have featured a seemingly endless string of internal political crises. Iraq's independent monarchical (1932–1958) and postrevolutionary (1958 to the present) periods have both been characterized by the lack of a national consensus about what constitutes legitimate, central governing authority in the country. A military coup — the first in the modern Middle East — deposed the Iraqi government in 1936 and inaugurated a period of instability in the second half of the 1930s. Uprisings against pro-British governments occurred in 1941, 1948, 1952, and 1956, before Prime Minister Nuri Said and the Hashemite monarchy were liquidated in the revolution of 1958. The 15 years following the revolution were plagued by incessant unrest and numerous coup attempts. Successful coups took place in 1963 (twice) and 1968 (a two-phased event), and another leadership change occurred in 1966 following the death of Abdel Salam Arif in a helicopter crash. The Ba'th Party, which gained control for a second time in 1968, faced repeated violent challenges to its authority before consolidating control of the country by about 1974.

The military was used as a bargaining chip in politics even before Iraq gained independence from Britain in 1932. Following the death of King Faisal I in 1933, ambitious officers turned the army into the preeminent political force in the country. The coups of the 1930s bequeathed to the army a legacy of activism in domestic affairs that became particularly significant in postrevolutionary Iraqi politics. Decisive military intervention brought political power to Abdel Karim Qasim, to the Ba'th Party in early 1963, to Abdel Salam Arif, and to the Ba'th again in 1968. Only since the mid-1970s, thanks to the domination of civilian Ba'this in the ruling councils of the party, has there been an effective check against the army's involvement in domestic politics.

*Rule by Political "Strong Man"*

True to its centuries-old reputation of being notoriously difficult to govern, modern Iraq has been ruled by a succession of forceful, if not openly dictatorial, men. King Faisal I, Iraq's first monarch, is the major unifying figure in Iraq's

history. He embodied both British and Iraqi nationalist aspirations for a united Iraq, and until his death in 1933, he
deftly manipulated the nascent political institutions of the
country toward that end. But no one picked up where
Faisal left off. The pro-British Nuri Said — a master of in-
trigue — was practiced at using brutal suppression when it
suited him. He effectively perpetuated his political control
through a corrupt clique of politicians until the collapse of
the monarchy in 1958. Each of the dictators that followed
the revolution — Abdel Karim Qasim, Abdel Salam Arif,
Abdel Rahman Arif, and Ahmad Hasan al-Bakr — left his
mark, but each also showed that conspiracy and military
force alone cannot sustain political control in Iraq.

Although Iraqi President Saddam Hussein as an op-
pressor and conspirator has much in common with his predecessors, he is no run-of-the-mill Iraqi strong man. His longevity as the premier power broker in Iraq since the early
1970s and his success in eliminating military intervention
in politics and institutionalizing Ba'thi influence are just
two reasons that he is the preeminent figure in postrevolutionary Iraqi politics. Nevertheless, definitive judgment on
Saddam's ultimate historical niche must await the outcome
of the war with Iran.

*Absence of Clear National Identity*

"In Iraq," wrote King Faisal shortly before his death,

> there is still . . . no Iraqi people but unimaginable
> masses of human beings, devoid of any patriotic idea,
> imbued with religious traditions and absurdities, con-
> nected by no common tie, . . . prone to anarchy, and
> perpetually ready to rise against any government
> whatever.[2]

The ethnic, religious, and regional divisions to which Faisal
referred have continued to plague Iraq and impede the development of a sense of national community. Historically,

Iraq was riven by the wide economic, social, and psychological gulf that separated urban Iraqis from rural tribal dwellers. This gulf has diminished, but not disappeared, in recent decades when the ascendant concern has been the tripartite segmentation of the country into Kurdish, Arab Sunni, and Arab Shi'a communities. Between 15 and 20 percent of Iraqis are Kurds, whose persistent separatism has unsettled nearly every central regime in the postwar era and caused a bloody civil war in 1974–1975. By contrast, Iraq's Shi'a majority (55 to 60 percent of the population) has no enduring tradition of political activism. Still, this did not prevent its minority Sunni leadership from attempting to blunt the call of Shi'a revolutionism from Iran. Nevertheless, the long years of fighting against Iran seem to have bequeathed a stronger sense of national community to Iraq. The potential reversal of the disintegrative influence of subnational tendencies is perhaps the most important long-term political prospect generated by the war.

*Regional and International Isolation*

For much of its life as a nation-state Iraq has been something of a pariah in its foreign relations. Iraqi and Syrian regimes from the 1940s on have alternately called for unification of the two countries and exchanged charges of complicity in attempted coups d'etat—a love-hate relationship typified in the bitter cycle of Iraqi-Syrian relations from 1978 to the present. Iraq's pan-Arab ambitions have also led to continuing tension with Egypt, which left Iraq isolated regionally for many of the years that Nasser's magnetism dominated Arab politics. Iraqi-Saudi relations were also strained for decades. Before 1958, Saudi-Hashemite dynastic rivalry engendered constant Saudi suspicion of Iraqi conspiracies to overthrow the Saudi monarchy, suspicions that the revolutionary rhetoric of Iraq's post-1958 regimes did little to dissipate.

## Impediments in U.S. policy toward Iraq, 1945–1975

The United States has found it similarly difficult to develop constructive relations with postwar Iraq. There are several reasons for this difficulty, but perhaps none is more fundamental than the persistent problems associated with Iraq's internal political situation. A recent conversation with a seasoned policy analyst and strategic thinker about Iraq's potential importance to U.S. policy was punctuated by his judgment that Iraq is "not even a real country," an apparent reference to its communal divisions and inconclusive sense of national identity. As a rationale for restraining U.S. policy interest in Iraq, this statement is backed by a lengthy tradition. Even in the early 1940s the State Department wanted to avoid close involvement with Iraq because of the "messiness" of its domestic politics.[3]

Nevertheless, as a frame of reference, it is important to note that U.S. policymakers at one point entertained high hopes for ties with Iraq. A State Department policy memorandum of February 1946 concluded: "It will be increasingly necessary for us to maintain closer relations with Iraq, since our standing in the entire area will to a considerable degree be dependent on the attitude of Iraq toward the United States."[4] This evaluation had surfaced in earlier memoranda and had ample opportunity for internal review, which suggests that serious consideration was given to the proposition that U.S. influence in the postwar Middle East would hinge "to a considerable degree" on U.S.-Iraqi relations.[5] In fact, though, almost nothing could have been further from the truth. In the decades after 1945, U.S. policy gave few countries in the Middle East more marginal consideration than Iraq. The plight of the Palestinians and events associated with Israel's birth as a state in 1948 frustrated the early development of common interests between Baghdad and Washington. Later, after conclusion of a military assistance agreement in 1954 and during the Baghdad Pact years of 1955–1958, U.S. relations with Iraq appeared to bloom briefly and to take on some importance. But the bloody coup of July 1958 in Baghdad quickly put an end to this positive trend.

A somewhat coarse example of bilateral "diplomacy" reveals something of the underlying, suspicious tone of U.S.-Iraqi relations in these early years. Just before the outbreak of the Arab-Israeli war of May 1948, Iraq was rocked by political instability. A prolonged wheat shortage and high bread prices maintained a crisis atmosphere for months. The November 1947 UN vote to partition Palestine and a hasty attempt by the monarchical regime to conclude a new treaty with Britain escalated tensions even further. Meanwhile, officials at the State Department seethed over reports of the infiltration of Iraqi troops into Palestine. By April, U.S. diplomats in Baghdad had reported economic and political conditions in Iraq that were "seriously disturbing" – grain production at a fraction of normal levels, widespread hunger, pervasive unemployment, communist activism, and no government funds to carry out needed programs. Under these circumstances, Iraq requested U.S. support for an emergency grain shipment and consideration of direct financial assistance. The chilling response from Washington instructed the U.S. ambassador to convey the "deep concern" of the United States to the Iraqi government, but added: "You should, however, point out that while USGovt is sincerely desirous of being of assistance, it would be difficult for USGovt to give consideration to appropriate measures in this respect as long as Palestine question remains unsettled."[6]

After 1958 and the advent of radical, revolutionary regimes in Baghdad, the general hostility between U.S. and Iraqi foreign policy interests expanded. Iraq immediately began to forge close ties with the Soviet Union, which culminated in the conclusion of a Soviet-Iraqi friendship treaty in 1972. There also appeared to be a stiffening of Iraq's already harsh attitude toward Israel. Baghdad's heated rhetoric rejected any diplomatic solution to the Arab-Israeli conflict and insisted on a military struggle to the end against "the Zionist entity." This zeal acquired concrete meaning for U.S.-Iraqi relations when Iraq joined with several other Arab countries to break diplomatic relations over U.S. support for Israel in the June 1967 war. Iraq did not agree to restore these ties until November 1984, long after the frontline Arab states had done so, and this lengthy hiatus stunted the development of understanding and common interests between Iraq and the United States.

Baghdad's policies in the Arab world were also a source of friction. For example, Iraq threatened in 1970 to invade Jordan to assist PLO forces in their conflict with King Hussein. This threat ultimately proved to be empty, but not before President Nixon had sent some 1,500 troops to Lebanon, a move that was directly and ominously reminiscent of Eisenhower's response to the Iraqi revolution in 1958. In addition, Iraq strenuously opposed the U.S. "twin pillars" strategy of arming Iran and Saudi Arabia to help protect U.S. interests in the Gulf. Finally, Washington also took umbrage with Iraq's active support (in the early 1970s) of groups committed to overthrowing the conservative Arab regimes in the Gulf.

Besides Iraq's political unpredictability and conflicting foreign policy objectives, there is a third important reason that Iraqi-U.S. relations have remain largely undeveloped. It is that Iraq has rarely, if ever, been of vital importance to the major regional initiatives undertaken by the United States in the postwar Middle East. For example, Iraq has never figured significantly in the numerous U.S. efforts to help resolve the Arab-Israeli conflict. Iraq's overheated rhetoric has always been contradicted by its geographic remoteness to the border with Israel. When it did join the fighting in 1948, 1967, and 1973, Iraq's involvement had little military significance. Yet Baghdad made a point of distancing itself from the agreements that ended these wars, reinforcing the impression that Iraq was peripheral to the resolution of the Arab-Israeli conflict.

Much the same could be said of U.S. regional strategies to contain Soviet influence and secure oil supplies from the

Gulf to the West. In the 1950s, Iraq was one of the "northern tier" countries identified by Secretary of State John
Foster Dulles for inclusion in a pro-Western alliance to
block Soviet access to the Middle East. Although Iraq
helped catalyze the formalization of that alliance as the
Baghdad Pact, U.S. policies clearly marked Iraq as the
least significant member of the grouping. Unlike Turkey
and Iran, Iraq did not border directly on the Soviet Union.
It also lacked the demographic and military resources of
Turkey, Iran, and Pakistan, three countries with which the
United States consequently went to great lengths to develop serious aid and political relationships. Iraq, however,
was sorely disappointed in the amount of U.S. military support it received as a member of the Baghdad Pact. Moreover, right up to the July 1958 revolution, Washington never broke from the pattern of deferring to British political
influence in Iraq.[7]

Finally, as already mentioned, Iraq opposed the U.S.
strategy to protect Western interests in the Gulf in the
1970s. This twin pillars policy, which hinged on the regional
influence of the shah's Iran (and secondarily on Saudi Arabia) to maintain stability in this key oil-producing region,
had as one of its cardinal tenets the exclusion of Iraq. Thus,
Iraq has consistently "fallen between the cracks" in the
regional plans developed by U.S. policymakers for the postwar Middle East. This condition of marginality, in turn, is
perhaps a major reason why greater effort was not expended to develop common U.S.-Iraqi interests to counteract the differences described above.


**Iraq before the War**

These brief summaries point up the difficulties that afflicted Iraqi political life and U.S.-Iraqi relations up to the mid-
1970s. To examine how the Gulf war has affected these
trends requires delving more deeply into the circumstances
that prevailed in Iraq in the years just before the war. The

last half of the 1970s was a time of tremendous change for Iraq, as the following list of article titles from this period attests:

"Iraq Turns Sour on Russia, and It's U.S. That Gains";
"Iraq Starts to Thaw";
"In Iraq, The East Is a Little Less Red";
"Iraq: An End to Isolationism, As Saddam Hussein Consolidates His Power";
"Surrounded by Turmoil, Iraq Is Shifting Its Posture";
"Iraq – New Power in the Middle East"; and
"Iraq: The West's Opportunity."[8]

One of the most startling changes in Iraq became evident by the mid-to-late 1970s – the imposition of a measure of political stability by the Ba'th. Saddam Hussein and the party's civilian wing institutionalized Ba'thi influence at all levels and in all sectors of Iraqi society. They also set up a pervasive security network outside the military and established a large party militia to offset the strength of the regular army. Scholars acknowledge that although these achievements did not permanently address the regime's underlying problem of legitimacy, they did succeed in establishing strong central authority in one of the Third World's most fragmented and difficult-to-govern political systems.[9]

An important turning point in Iraq's fortunes was the collapse of the Iranian-backed Kurdish insurgency, which waged a bloody civil war against the central government in 1974–1975. Saddam Hussein and the shah of Iran initialed the Algiers accord in March 1975, which ended outside support for the Kurds and enabled Iraqi forces to overrun Kurdish positions in a matter of weeks. Although it did not end Kurdish opposition to the Ba'thi government, the agreement reduced the problem to manageable dimensions and paved the way for continued predominance by the Ba'th.

Iraq by the late 1970s was also reaping unprecedented benefits from its oil industry. The Ba'th gradually complet-

Saddam Hussein was the major catalyst in building the consensus that eventually expelled Egypt from the League and in so doing positioned Iraq to take over Egypt's leadership role. All in all, Iraq seemed to have transformed itself from a pariah into a regional power much to be reckoned with.

## The Blind Spot in U.S. Policy toward Iraq

Despite these changes in Iraq's policies and regional stature during the late 1970s, the United States did not change its basic policy toward Iraq. Iraq's foreign minister and the U.S. secretary of state consulted at the United Nations on a fairly regular basis, and several times during the Carter administration probes were made to determine whether the opportunity existed for a significant opening to Iraq. These efforts accomplished little.[13] Instead, the bilateral political climate continued to be dominated by the absence of bilateral diplomatic ties, Iraq's criticism of U.S. support for Israel, and lingering suspicions about earlier U.S. support for the Kurdish insurgency.

Saddam Hussein's activism in the Arab League councils that banished Egypt put Baghdad and Washington at odds over the top priority in Carter's Middle East policy — the Camp David accords. Furthermore, in 1979 Congress had placed Iraq on a list of countries accused of supporting acts of international terrorism. At this time, a negative image of the Iraqi regime as repressive on human rights also began to take hold in both official and unofficial circles in the United States. Overall, the most encouraging gesture that could be contrived between the two countries was for the White House and the State Department to affirm U.S. readiness to normalize relations with Iraq.[14]

The U.S. failure to respond with more alacrity to changes in Iraq in the 1970s exacerbated the weakness of its regional position following the Iranian revolution. The advent of the Khomeini regime provided ample food for thought about the need for greater U.S. awareness of and responsiveness to Iraq's evolving domestic and international bearing. And indeed, between 1980 and 1985, the lesson seemed to take hold, as many of the impediments that hindered U.S.-Iraqi relations in the Carter years were eliminated. Iraq was removed from the list of terrorism supporters in early 1982, and full diplomatic relations between Washington and Baghdad were restored in 1984. Iraq has also helped restore Egypt's standing in the Arab world. Saddam Hussein altered Iraq's unyielding opposition to a negotiated Arab settlement with Israel to acceptance of any formula agreed to by the Palestinians. Finally, there was the important evolution of a perception between Iraq and the United States that the prevention of Baghdad's defeat by Iran constituted a common strategic interest—the first such interest between the two countries since the Baghdad Pact.

But for all their exceptionality, the improvements in U.S.-Iraqi relations that culminated in the resumption of formal relations in 1984 were clearly overshadowed by U.S. and Israeli arms sales to Iran in 1985 and 1986. Baghdad's complaints about the sale of Western arms to Tehran grew in intensity following the withdrawal of Iraqi troops from Iran in 1982. After Iran rejected a UN ceasefire resolution late in 1983, the Reagan administration initiated "Operation Staunch," an effort to dissuade U.S. allies in Europe and elsewhere from transferring lethal military goods to Tehran. From 1984 to 1986, this campaign became an increasingly visible element of U.S. policy toward Iraq and the Gulf war. In one sense, it became the centerpiece of U.S. policy toward the war because it was an open, universally known attempt to exert a direct (albeit limited), constraining influence on the course of fighting.

Thus, the secret policy of selling arms to Iran reversed the basic thrust of U.S. policy toward the Iran-Iraq war in at least two ways. First, it undermined Operation Staunch, and second, it negated the posture of neutrality under which Washington had foresworn giving arms to either side since the beginning of the conflict. The overturning of these policy positions was completed when President Reagan avowed that ending the Iran-Iraq war had indeed been one of the primary objectives in pursuing arms sales to Iran.[15]

There are other substantial reasons (the effect on U.S. terrorism policy, for example) to criticize the U.S. and Israeli arms sales to Iran, but our focus here will be the implications for U.S. policy toward Iraq. Oddly enough, the many investigations and analyses—public and private— that unfolded in the months after the "Irangate" scandal was revealed in November 1986 devoted little if any attention to the arms sales as a betrayal of Iraq. Nevertheless, the implications of such an assessment of the scandal are of major significance.

Primarily, these implications center on the Reagan administration's evident willingness to dismiss the significance of the serious improvements that had been made in U.S.-Iraqi relations in the preceding years and its readiness to put Iraq at risk in its war with Iran—all in hopes of gaining an elusive "strategic opening" with some undefined, future regime in Tehran. Any useful assessment of past or prospective U.S. policy toward Iraq must look at more than the progress of political contacts and common interests (even strategic ones). It must also account for what is clearly an impoverished U.S. perception of the good Iraq can ultimately do for U.S. interests in the region.

Perhaps the best way to illustrate the deficiency in the U.S. estimation of Iraq's regional importance to U.S. interests is to examine certain parallels between Irangate and the last time Iraq was at the center of a major foreign policy crisis for the United States. This took place in 1958, when a revolutionary coup in Iraq overthrew the pro-Western monarchy and "touched off a full-blown world crisis involving the prospect of staggering loss to the Western position in the Middle East and the risk of a major war."[16] Before 1958 (as during the mid-1980s) Iraq and the United States appeared to share a common goal of overriding strategic significance. During 1954 and 1955, Iraq played a catalytic role in the formation of the Baghdad Pact, which fulfilled John Foster Dulles's vision of a "northern tier" alliance to contain the Soviet Union.[17] But ultimately, the United States itself did not join the pact, leaving Great Britain as its sole Western adherent. Furthermore, the Eisenhower administration also secretly discouraged other Arab states from acceding to it and failed to provide the extensive military assistance that Baghdad expected to receive for becoming a link in the pro-Western northern tier.[18]

The historical record now shows that a central objective of Washington's cool treatment of monarchical Iraq was to placate Nasser.[19] At the time, Nasser's policies were clearly contradictory to Western interests, but his eventual cooperation was deemed vital to strategic U.S. aims in the Middle East. In short, by leaving Iraq exposed and isolated in the Baghdad Pact, the United States put Iraq's position in the region at risk for the sake of a long-shot opening with a hostile, but strategically placed, regional power: Nasser's Egypt. Only with the collapse of the Iraqi monarchy in 1958, which precipitated one of the most disruptive crises ever for Western interests in the Middle East, did it become clear what the United States had risked by putting less emphasis on cultivating the pro-Western status quo in Iraq than on pursuing a low-percentage opening with a large, but basically hostile, regional power.

This digression into the somewhat distant past suggests an enduring blind spot in U.S. policy toward Iraq. Two serious postwar crises involving threats to the status quo in Iraq—the 1958 revolution and the threat of an Iranian defeat of Iraq in the 1980s—have caught U.S. policymakers leaning away from fulfillment of public commitments to vulnerable regimes in Baghdad. In each instance, a calculation was made that Iraq's limited regional significance made it advisable to equivocate on these commitments to appease the regional powerhouses—Nasser's Egypt and Khomeini's Iran. The damage done to Western interests by the Iraqi revolution of 1958 should have pre-

vented the United States from blindly repeating its minimalist calculus of Iraq in the 1980s, but it did not. The
discussion in the following chapters is offered in the perhaps stubborn hope that it might help prevent this mistake
from occurring a third time.

# 2

# Forging a National Consensus: The Political Consolidation of Iraq

But whether [the] regime will stand out historically hinges, in the long run, upon its ability to contribute, in a creative manner, to the process of nation-state building. . . .

—Hanna Batatu

For the first time since the death of King Faisal I in 1933, an Iraqi regime had appeared that seemed to have the potential to make a historic contribution to the consolidation of the Iraqi state. This opinion was the thrust of several analyses, including the one cited above, of the Iraqi Ba'th Party in the late 1970s. The Ba'th had vast economic resources at its disposal; it had imposed a forceful, but not airtight, authority structure; and the Kurdish insurrection was well in hand. A breakthrough in Iraq's history of chronic political instability and rejection of centralized authority seemed possible, if not yet imminent. Studies of Iraq completed in recent years look to these prewar circumstances as a reference point, a high-water mark that the invasion of Iran rendered all but meaningless. The war, the studies suggest, has completely undone the best hope for genuine national progress in Iraq.[1]

But this is not necessarily so. As destructive and malevolent as the war has been, it has reemphasized some fundamental questions that might never have been directly addressed except during a time of serious national stress: Does Iraq really exist as a focus of primary political loyalty for its people? Is a stable government with a central authority viable? Can the military be relied upon to defend the political status quo? After all, Iran has tested Iraq at some allegedly very vulnerable points. It has flaunted its own revolutionary success in front of Iraq's perpetually underprivileged Shi'a majority, personally assailed Saddam Hussein as a secular and elitist dictator, and challenged a military force that by tradition is more prone to unseating Iraqi regimes than protecting them. But Iraq has held its ground against this withering political and military assault, which suggests that a reexamination of basic assumptions about Iraq's politics is in order.

## Iraqi National Consciousness

The genesis and development of the Iran-Iraq war have raised three fundamental concerns about Iraqi politics: the tension between the national and sectarian or ethnic loyalties of Iraq's Shi'a and Kurdish communities; the concentration of political power in the hands of Iraq's President Saddam Hussein; and the relationship between Iraq's political leadership and the expanded and traditionally interventionist military. Focusing on these three variables, the following discussion attempts to trace how the war has affected these important underlying features of Iraqi politics. It will become apparent that the influence of the conflict on political evolution in Iraq has perhaps not been altogether negative.

The effect of the war on national cohesion and identity has by almost all accounts been overridingly positive. The social cement that tenuously held Iraq together in the past has not dissolved, nor apparently even weakened, under duress. If anything, the bonds have grown stronger. The best evidence of this development is that the large majority of Iraq's Shi'is have not responded to Iranian calls for the overthrow of the Ba'thi regime. This reality has wide repercussions. Regionally, the absence of a Shi'a uprising in Iraq has given the lie to Ayatollah Khomeini's dismissal of national boundaries as impediments to his Islamic revolution. Because they make up a decisive majority of the population but occupy a back seat in the Sunni-dominated political and economic order, Iraq's 7 to 8 million Shi'is were believed ripe for a Khomeini-inspired rebellion. Instead, their firmness has generated suggestions that Iraq's Shi'a community has experienced "a triumph of national feelings over religious ones."[2] If so, and if it can be made permanent, that triumph could be a most important breakthrough in Iraq's decades-long quest for a strong national identity.

*Saddam's Prewar Shi'a Policies*

The political restiveness of the Shi'a community has been a source of concern for the Ba'thi regime since 1969, but it emerged as a national dilemma when Saddam Hussein seized power in 1977–1979.[3] By several accounts, Saddam rode into office on the crest of an internal Ba'th Party crisis precipitated by Shi'a unrest and a dispute over whether to accommodate Ba'thi doctrine to the Islamic resurgence.[4] This historical background suggests the importance Saddam has ascribed to the regime's Shi'a policies and his perception that the viability of Ba'thi rule, and his own, is closely tied to those policies.

Saddam's prewar policies toward Iraq's Shi'is established several lasting dichotomies. He drew a sharp distinction between the brutal treatment meted out to Iraq's militant Shi'a *'ulama* and the underground extremists of the al-Da'wa Party, and accommodation of the Shi'a populace in general. His attitudes about Shi'is participating in Ba'th Party politics were also segmented: he blocked Shi'a involvement at the upper echelons but sought to expand the political options of the Shi'is at lower, less threatening lev-

els. Finally, it is useful for purposes of illustration to juxta-
pose these political aspects of Saddam's policy with attempts to reach Iraq's Shi'is through economic and cultural
means. The following vignettes attempt to flesh out these
dichotomies.

*The War with al-Da'wa.* In the 14 months before September 1980 (the time span between Saddam's first record-
ed remark that Iraq might need to invade Iran to prevent a
Shi'a uprising and the actual invasion of Iran), the Iraqi
regime undertook a vigorous campaign against al-Da'wa
and executed large numbers of its members and supporters.[5] The regime and al-Da'wa were almost at war during this period, with the latter carrying out terrorist attacks and assassination attempts against government
officials. One sequence of events – an April 1, 1980 attempt
to kill second Deputy Prime Minister Tariq Aziz and a subsequent bombing of the crowd mourning victims of the first
attack – was pivotal in the downward spiral of Iraqi-Iranian
recriminations that led to the outbreak of the war.

*Repression of Hard-Core 'Ulama.* To quell unrest after
Khomeini's takeover in Iran and reportedly to prevent a trip
to Iran for the purpose of congratulating Khomeini, Saddam imprisoned Ayatollah Muhammad Baqir al-Sadr in
June 1979.[6] Sadr, a long-time associate of Khomeini who
was deemed to be the Iraqi equivalent of Khomeini in both
charisma and religious authority, had sought to expand his
network of religious influence throughout Iraq from his
base in Najaf. His imprisonment caused further rioting,
leading to the crisis that resulted in Saddam's accession to
the presidency in July. In April 1980, just days after the
attempt on Tariq Aziz's life, Sadr was executed, the first
instance in which a modern Iraqi regime dared to execute a
leading Shi'a cleric.[7]

*Mass Deportations.* Saddam Hussein also ordered the
expulsion of large numbers of politically suspect Shi'is
whom the regime claimed were Iranian in origin. Estimates

vary widely as to how many individuals were expelled by
Iraq. The figure of 30,000 should probably be considered a
minimum; claims as high as 350,000 have been made.[8] Iran
has set as a condition for ending the war that Iraq must
accept repatriation of 200,000 Iraqi exiles now in Iran.[9]

*Political Access for the Shi'is.* From the 1968 coup
until September 1977, the Ba'th Revolutionary Command
Council (RCC), the paramount political body in Iraq, had
not a single Shi'a among its members. By the beginning of
the war with Iran, Shi'is still occupied a marginal position
in the regime's ruling council. Beginning in about 1977,
however, the Ba'th began a vigorous campaign to attract
Shi'is to its general membership, with some apparent success. Furthermore, in June 1980, Saddam convened elections for a National Assembly, the first national poll in
postrevolutionary Iraq. Given the tight controls on Iraqi
politics, the results of this election (40 percent of its elected
members were Shi'a, as was its appointed speaker, Naim
Haddad) strongly suggest that a primary reason for setting
up the National Assembly was to provide an outlet (however subdued) for Shi'a political energies.[10]

*Religious and Economic Palliatives.* Although Saddam vigorously rejected the adoption of Islamic strictures
into Ba'th Party ideology, he hastened to add that there
were no inherent contradictions between the two.[11] He also
made a point of invoking symbols and identifying with historical personalities in a manner that would resonate with
Shi'is. Shi'a commemorations that had been ignored for decades were now celebrated. Government funds flowed to support *'ulama* who disagreed sharply with Baqir al-Sadr's activist politics and were willing to voice open support for the
regime. Money was expended to renovate Sunni and Shi'a
religious shrines alike, which Saddam and other Ba'thi officials visited with increasing frequency.[12] Finally, the regime
channeled industrial and other economic development projects into Iraq's southern Shi'a areas as a way to spread the
economic benefits of the country's oil boom.[13]

*The Shi'a Issue during the War*

During the war Saddam has kept up the carrot-and-stick approach with the Shi'a community. The regime's battles with militant Iraqi Shi'is have continued, parallel to and often closely synchronized with the fight against Iran. The 1982 establishment of the Supreme Assembly of the Islamic Revolution of Iraq (SAIRI), a Shi'a government-in-exile based in Tehran, followed quickly on the heels of Iraqi troops' forced withdrawal from Iran. Al-Da'wa and other extremist groups (most notably the Organization for Islamic Action) perpetrated bloody attacks on government installations in Baghdad in 1982, 1983, and 1984.

Since the war began, al-Da'wa is also credited with at least two major assassination attempts against Iraqi officials. In July 1982, Saddam and his entourage were pinned down for several hours at the village of Dujayl, 40 miles northeast of Baghdad. Assassins reportedly slew a number of presidential bodyguards before rescuers arrived and killed the attackers. Overall casualties were estimated at 150, and the village (apparently the site of an earlier attack on Saddam) was later razed and its inhabitants dispersed.[14] In September 1987, a similar attack occurred at the town of Baquba, also north of Baghdad, while Iraqi dignitaries and foreign diplomats reviewed an official parade. The 50 to 100 people who were reportedly killed during the assault and the firing that ensued included children and officials of the Ba'th Party. The incident clearly seemed designed to undermine the regime's image of unassailable control in the eyes of the foreign audience.[15]

The government's response to al-Da'wa's predations has been severe. In 1983, it arrested about 100 members of a prominent clerical family, the al-Hakim, executing 6 or 7 of them that year and 10 more in 1985. It reportedly has arrested family members (including women and children) of suspected al-Da'wa adherents. Membership in al-Da'wa and similar groups is punishable by death, and in 1983 (one of the most difficult years of the war for Iraq) some 300 extremists may have been executed. In addition, the Ba'thi People's Army has spread a vast security net across southern Iraq. Meanwhile, the government has also sharply expanded its control over religious affairs by taking charge of revenues, clergy appointments, religious literature, and the maintenance of shrines.[16]

Saddam has also continued to dispense economic favors and symbolic religious gestures to the Shi'a community and has granted visibly better Shi'a access to the upper rungs of the political system. Following the June 1982 Regional Congress of the Ba'th, changes were made in the party's Regional Command (or RC, the second most powerful body in the country) that left it with a plurality, if not a majority, of Shi'a members. These new members also widened the RC's geographic base to include representation from the Shi'a holy cities of Najaf and Karbala.[17] The Shi'a south has been a prime beneficiary of the "guns and butter" policy that laid out large economic development expenditures well into the war. Social services have expanded accordingly, markedly improving the overall economic and social status of the Shi'a community. Finally, the regime has invested perhaps as much as a quarter of a billion dollars to renovate the main shrines in Najaf and Karbala. It has convened a series of international conferences on Islam in Baghdad, and individual regime leaders have been visibly more inclined to demonstrations of religious piety as well.[18]

The carrot-and-stick explanation for Shi'a quiescence has evident appeal but equally evident limitations. Its appeal derives in large part from the fact that the regime's dealings with the Shi'a community — that is, the physical intimidations and material inducements — are tangible, observable phenomena. Much more difficult to address, particularly in Iraq's closed society, are nontangible, psychological questions. Is a sense of national loyalty and identity developing, for example, among the members of this important religious subgroup? An answer to this question is necessarily impressionistic, but nevertheless indispensable.

Why? Because to many close observers of Iraq, the carrot-and-stick metaphor has worn thin as a comprehensive explanation, now that Iraqi Shi'is have stood firmly at the forefront of the military and political conflict with Iran for more than seven years. Observers find it hardly credible to accept that, over this period of time and under these circumstances, Iraq's 7 to 8 million Shi'is have been cowed into permanent passivity purely by repression or material bribes by the regime.

The search for a more complete explanation of Shi'a communal quiescence during the war involves several variables. There is, for example, the basic question of how deeply many Iraqi Shi'is feel their religion. One careful observer noted early in the war that the Shi'is who had migrated from the countryside to the slums of Baghdad were an unlikely focus for religious incitement. The reasons for this included the feeble organization of religion in the rural areas where these migrants originated; their tribal and bedouin roots, which implied neither a tendency to religious ardor nor a rigorous grounding in Shi'a dogma; and their likely preference for tribal custom over Islamic stricture of either the Shi'a or Sunni variety.[19]

Researchers have also invoked historical, geographical, and organizational reasons for the nonappearance of a serious or widespread Shi'a opposition movement. One writer has stressed that unlike the Kurds, Iraqi Shi'a have no history of strong political leadership or organized military struggle, and no well-defined political agenda. The Shi'a south is also physically much more susceptible to government control than the mountains of Kurdistan.[20] Another scholar has suggested that since the late 1920s, a substantial number of leading Shi'a clerics in Iraq have opposed direct religious intervention in politics. This tendency was reinforced in the late 1970s when the activist Muhammad Baqir al-Sadr alienated many of the local *ulama* throughout Iraq by attempting to supplant them with his own emissaries from Najaf. Moreover, the fact that religious students from the holy Shi'a cities are exempted from mili-

tary service has prevented communications between militant religious leaders and Iraqi soldiers, which helps explain the military's cohesion behind the government during
the war.[21]

The key question to which these considerations all
point is: How strong are national loyalty and identity
among Iraq's Shi'is? This question has been the central
political issue facing Iraq since the emergence of Khomeini's Shi'a revolution in Iran. Has the war decisively
shown that, politically speaking, Iraq's Shi'is are Iraqi and
Arab before they are Shi'a? Are they committed, or at least
predictably content, to forge a political identity in the context of a secular Iraqi nation-state? Although not all analysts agree that the war has settled the question, it is tell-
ing that they all seem to accept it as a possibility—in some
cases, quite grudgingly. Note, for example, the following
self-styled interim assessment of Khomeini's impact on the
Iraqi Shi'a community.

> So far, Khomeyni's relentless and undisguised efforts
> to export the Islamic revolution to Iraq by way of the
> Shi'is have failed dismally. The Iraqi regime's tight grip
> and the Shi'is' weak organization and passivity, as
> well as, *perhaps*, their sense of loyalty to the Iraqi-
> Arab nation state are primary causes for Khomeyni's
> failure.[22]

Hanna Batatu, on the other hand, suggested that after
only a few months the war was sharpening for Iraqi Shi'is a
sense of Arab-Iranian differentness, "particularly for those
who have all along held that their Arab or Iraqi identity is
more important than their Shi'a or Islamic affiliation."
Batatu also injected a note of caution concerning al-Da'wa's
close identification with Iran.

> "In their heart of hearts," as one dedicated Shi'i put it to
> this writer recently, "Iraq's Shi'is like things to grow
> from their own soil." This is why they took so much
> pride in Baqir Muhammad al-Sadr, who, they felt, was

one of theirs and the only Arab among the eight Shi'a
*marji's* [or ayatollahs] of the day. Moreover, at least in
the past it was possible to sense in Najaf itself an un-
dercurrent of tension between Iranian and Arab "*'ulama*". . . . Iraq's Shi'is are clearly more comfortable
with their own kind and prefer that real leadership
should be in the hands of Shi'is that are Iraqi.[23]

When they were published in 1981, Batatu's comments
seemed somewhat out of place. Before Iraq's predominant-
ly Shi'a troops withdrew from Iran in 1982, their lackluster
performance had been blamed in part on divided loyalties.
The periodic reports that described the desertion of large
numbers of Shi'a soldiers were most likely exaggerated, but
indicated the underlying concern.[24] Following the withdrawal and Iraq's successful defense of Basra, the tone of
analysis changed dramatically. Writers now spoke of *Iraq's*
"patriotic fervor" and declared, "Now it is Tehran which
plays the dangerous game of pinning military hopes on an
internal revolt." These hopes were depicted as foundering
on the quietude of Iraq's Shi'is, who reportedly had little
sense of communal consciousness and now were vulnerable
to "Arab nationalist appeals against the Persians."[25]

Since 1982, repeated Iranian offensives, terrorism by
al-Da'wa, and appeals from the SAIRI exiles in Iran have
all failed to disrupt the fundamental stability of Iraq's Shi'a
community. In 1983, some Shi'is reportedly appealed to
Khomeini to stop the war because of the rising death toll of
young Iraqi Shi'a soldiers.[26] Their appeal indicated that, by
this time, elements among the Shi'a faithful had begun to
transfer blame for the war from Saddam Hussein to Khomeini. By 1984, this had become a widespread pattern.

The excesses and outrageous behavior of Tehran's religious leaders have . . . been a powerful factor in damaging the Islamic Republic's reputation not just among
Iraqi Sunnis and Christians, but also among the more
moderate Shias of Najaf and Kerbala who want no part
of the lot of their fellow Muslims in Iran. Imam Kho-

meini has become a convenient bugaboo which the Iraqi authorities invoke all day long to encourage the people to close ranks around their regime.[27]

A similar report updated the state of affairs to mid-1986:

> The regime's sins of commission in beginning the war are swallowed up by the Iranian offense in attacking Iraq after the withdrawal of Iraqi troops from Iran in 1982. The defectors who live in Iran are badly received in Iraq and the dissident Shia groups have made remarkably little progress inside Iraq as a mass movement.[28]

Despite such assessments, until the war ends, and perhaps even for some time thereafter, the possibility cannot be permanently discounted that the Shi'is will rise up against the Ba'thi government. At the same time, it is not too early to suggest that much of the debate about the Iraqi Shi'a community is superficial and unjustifiably pessimistic. A balanced approach would note that numerous assessments, drawn from a variety of respectable sources and time periods, emphasize and reemphasize the Shi'a disinclination to abandon the Iraqi state. Hence, if policy analysis concerning present-day (or even post-Gulf war) Iraq requires a working hypothesis on this question, the war has probably exerted a decisive, consolidating influence on Iraqi politics by cementing the national loyalty of Iraq's Shi'is. In light of their sustained and firm support for the political and military struggle to survive the war with Iran, the proposition must be considered that the vast majority of Iraqi Shi'a support the Iraqi state and the cause of secular nationalism that it embodies.

*The Kurdish Factor*

There is less optimism, however, concerning the war's effect on nationalist sentiment in Iraq's Kurdish community. Although it has appeared at times during the war that internal divisiveness and governmental accommodation would blunt the effect of Kurdish separatism, these hopes were short-lived. Indeed, by the end of 1986 and early 1987, all positive contacts had broken off between Saddam Hussein's regime and the Kurdish insurgents, who had apparently formed at least a tactical, antiregime alliance among themselves and thus posed, for the first time since the war began, their maximum threat to the Iraqi regime.

The seeds of both the hope and frustration that have beset the Kurdish issue during the war were sown by the policies pursued after 1975. Kurdistan was relatively quiet in the half-decade that followed the civil war. The central government implemented a vigorous program of economic development and land reform, bringing social and economic benefits to many of northern Iraq's Kurdish inhabitants. At the same time, however, a harsh resettlement campaign begun in 1976 removed tens of thousands of Kurds from the northern Iran-Iraq frontier. Tribes that were politically suspect and progovernment suffered alike under the operation, and the resentment it caused provided the impetus for Kurdish groups to resume small-scale guerrilla actions against the government. The two main Kurdish separatist movements — the Kurdish Democratic Party, or KDP, and the Patriotic Union of Kurdistan, or PUK, led by Jalal Talabani — reestablished themselves in Kurdistan during this period. Nevertheless, violent infighting and the regional economic boom stunted the movement's appeal.[29]

Nor did matters change quickly when the Iran-Iraq war began. The fighting caused the Iraqi regime to reduce its troop strength in Kurdistan and allow Kurdish exiles in the south to return to camps in the north, from which many escaped into border areas now controlled by the KDP.[30] Still, these developments only served to intensify the scope of KDP-PUK hostility. Despite the infusion of support from Iran and Syria, Kurdish efforts to build an effective anti-governmental coalition in the first two years of the war faltered.[31]

But circumstances for Iraq's Kurdish dissidents began

to change in 1983, as the regime reeled under the effect of
Iran's expulsion of Iraqi troops and a major economic crisis. Early in the year Kurdish deserters were offered amnesty and the option to do their military service in the
north, away from the Iran-Iraq war zone—an indication
that desertions had become a serious problem for the Ba'thi
government. Reportedly, Saddam Hussein at this time
opened secret discussions with the full range of Kurdish
dissident groups—another indication of the regime's sense
of vulnerability.[32] But the promise of these talks, if any, had
little opportunity to mature. Turkey was expressing its
misgivings to Baghdad about intrusions into the border
zone under KDP control, which were provoking unrest in
its Kurdish areas. Because it could do nothing about these
incursions, the Iraqi government agreed to waive the in-
violability of its borders following a May raid that killed
several Turkish soldiers. As a result, thousands of Turkish
troops crossed into Iraqi territory for a cleanup operation
lasting several days. The official account of this unprecedented action minimized the fighting and casualties involved. Kurdish sources, however, claimed that several
hundred of its partisans were killed or wounded and expressed fear that a far-reaching Turkish-Iraqi campaign
against the Kurds had begun.[33]

The KDP lost no time responding in kind to the threat
it perceived. When Iran extended the active war front to
northern Iraq in July and October 1983, KDP *Pesh Mergas*
("those who face death") joined the invading forces. In the
July attack, KDP forces retook Hajj Umran, the mountain
stronghold from which Mustafa Barzani's men had been
driven in 1975. Symbolically, this was a poignant reasser-
tion by Barzani's sons of the family's decades-long struggle
against a central government in Iraq. More concretely, the
KDP had reportedly acquired some relatively sophisticated
weaponry through Iran and used it to good effect. Dissident Iraqi Shi'as were also reported to have moved up from
the southern front to join the fray, fostering what proved to
be unfounded speculation that "a strategic alliance" was

forming among Iraqi opposition groups that might pose a serious threat to Saddam Hussein from within.[34]

The premature nature of these judgments became evident as Jalal Talabani and the PUK resisted the KDP-Iranian advances, at times from positions already evacuated by the retreating Iraqi army. The social and political differences that had separated the KDP and PUK for years had been aggravated by the Barzanis' decision to support Iran's invasion and help the Khomeini regime suppress its own Kurdish uprising.[35] Now, under military pressure, Talabani was forced out of his frontier haven deeper into Iraq, where he quickly concluded a cease-fire agreement with Saddam Hussein while the government carried out harsh reprisals against suspected Barzani supporters.

Saddam Hussein and Jalal Talabani began negotiations on an overall settlement of the Kurdish autonomy issue in November 1983. These discussions, which lasted between five and ten months, constituted the war's most hopeful development in relations with the Kurds. From the beginning though, some viewed the talks as merely another short-lived accommodation, the likes of which various regimes and Kurdish parties had concluded "with monotonous regularity over the past 20 years."[36] From all indications, Talabani and the PUK undertook to negotiate, on behalf of all Iraqi Kurds, the kind of arrangement for which Kurdish separatist movements had been fighting for decades — one that provided for significant administrative, economic, and cultural autonomy in all of the Kurdish-dominated regions of northern Iraq. Among the provisions reportedly discussed were democratic elections for legislative and executive councils for the autonomous region; formation of a 40,000-member Kurdish defense force to "protect Kurdistan from foreign enemies"; expansion of the existing autonomous zone to include larger portions of the Kurdish-dominated areas of Iraq; and allocation of a fixed proportion (20–30 percent) of Kirkuk-generated oil revenues for reconstruction and economic development projects in Iraqi Kurdistan.[37]

In early 1984 it was reported on no fewer than four occasions that a signed agreement between the PUK and the government was about to be published. It never occurred. Instead, a deadlock in the negotiations took hold, following which clashes broke out between government security forces and Kurdish protestors in PUK-controlled areas. Thereafter the talks collapsed altogether. Although detailed reasons were not given, it was widely believed that the negotiations foundered on such issues as who should control the Kurdish security force, the level at which to fix oil revenues for Kurdistan, the return of Kurdish peasants to their homes along the frontiers with Turkey and Iran, and perhaps most important, whether Kirkuk should be included in the autonomous region. At one point a compromise was reported that provided for joint Arab-Kurdish-Turkoman administration of the city of Kirkuk and its immediate environs (the seat of Iraq's oldest and largest-producing oil facilities), while the remainder of Kirkuk province would be ceded to the autonomous zone.[38] Other theories that surfaced suggested that negotiations stalled because Saddam Hussein failed to get Iraq's ruling RCC to agree to the Kurdish demands; because the military and economic crises of 1983 had receded, reducing the government's need to make concessions; or possibly because the talks with Talabani were merely a ruse by Saddam to divide the Kurdish insurgency. At the same time, Turkey, on whom Iraq was completely dependent for a route to export its oil, wanted to undercut any significant concessions by Baghdad, which it feared would provoke restiveness within Turkey's much larger Kurdish community.[39]

It appeared at first that this sequence of events left Saddam Hussein as the big winner over the Kurdish dissident movements. Talabani was discredited for having consorted with the Iraqi regime: his long-standing support from Syria had been cut off, and up to a third of his PUK fighters had allegedly deserted to other groups.[40] Meanwhile, the Barzani-led KDP had failed to spark a broader Kurdish uprising from its symbolic outpost inside Iraqi territory; it was rejected in part because of its close collaboration with Iran.[41] Furthermore, it was believed that there remained "a considerable number of Kurds who [saw] their economic, if not their political, future in cooperation with the central government."[42] Nevertheless, there were others who viewed the break with Talabani as the loss of "a first-class opportunity" to "radically remold" the country's politics.[43] This assessment has acquired greater credibility with the progressive erosion of the government's position in Kurdistan in the intervening years.

Since 1984, the political and military potency of the Kurdish insurgency in Iraq has expanded notably, placing it in a position to become a major, perhaps even decisive, variable in the equation of the Iran-Iraq war. Following the resumption of hostilities with the PUK, Baghdad expanded the military's presence in Kurdistan and the scope of its attacks on Kurdish targets. Economic pressure was also brought to bear, and up to 150,000 Kurdish irregulars were reportedly conscripted to defend against threats from Iran and Kurdish separatists. But these measures had little effect.[44] Drawing inspiration and perhaps direct support from their Iraqi counterparts, Turkey's Kurdish rebels began their own campaign of attacks in August 1984 — first against military targets but later against civilian collaborators as well. This sparked another major operation by Turkish troops in Iraqi territory in October, accompanied by announcements in Ankara and Baghdad that the two countries had concluded an agreement to allow "hot pursuit" of guerrillas into each other's territory.[45]

These incidents seemed to signal a new phase in the evolution of wartime Iraq's Kurdish problem. They provoked a lengthy and impassioned condemnation from the PUK, Baghdad's erstwhile negotiating partner. Within months, Talabani's fighters were inflicting costly losses on the Iraqi military, appealing for help from Libya, and taking foreign hostages in an effort to bring international pressure to bear on the regime.[46] Turkey's cross-border foray was also followed suspiciously soon by a shakeup in the long-standing leadership of the Kurdistan Revolutionary Party, part of the Ba'th-led National and Patriotic Front.[47] Even the extreme Kurdish loyalists were having difficulty accepting the regime's approach.

More important, however, has been the gradual closing of ranks between the hitherto bitterly antagonistic KDP and PUK and their association with other major elements of the Iraqi opposition. Mas'ud Barzani of the KDP took the lead in this consolidation effort, which was directed at (among others) the PUK, the ICP, and al-Da'wa, and nurtured by Iran, Syria, and Libya. Although he initially met with only partial success, observers took note particularly of Iran's new willingness to deal with secular, even communist, opponents of Saddam.[48] On the other hand, Barzani's connections to the Khomeini regime continued to be a source of concern to the PUK, though it was no longer a fighting matter. Leaders from his own KDP also entertained suspicions, protesting Iran's construction of a strategic road into the midst of KDP-controlled territory and refusing to be drawn into frontal assaults alongside Iranian forces.[49]

But attitudes seemed to change as the KDP carved out further military successes on its own. By the beginning of 1986, the KDP had reportedly extended its area of control to nearly the entire length of the Iraq-Turkey border, which was also a haven for most other Iraqi dissident groups as well as the Kurdish Workers' Party (PKK), Turkey's main rebel group. The acquisition of modern weapons and artillery through Iran enabled the KDP to exert pressure on Iraqi military outposts in the north and to counteract the regime's helicopter gunships, a key tactical achievement.[50] Morale and recruitment were already at high levels early in 1986 when the KDP claimed a major victory at a town called Mangesh, close to the Turkey-Baghdad highway and pipeline. Fifteen hundred Iraqi troops were reportedly captured, and Saddam Hussein had to commit his crack Presidential Guards to contain the damage. Comments from Turkey and the KDP exuded sensitivity to the growing threat posed to the strategic highway and oil pipeline.[51]

These Kurdish gains in the north, it will be remembered, paralleled significant Iraqi setbacks elsewhere in the ground war with Iran: at Fao (February 1986) in the southern sector, and at Mehran (July 1986) in the central sector of the front. Matters appeared to take an even sharper turn in October. At that time, PUK *Pesh Mergas* reportedly led Iranian forces on strikes against two major economic installations deep inside northern Iraq, one of which was the central oil complex at Kirkuk. Although Iranian claims vastly exaggerated the amount of damage done, the operation appeared to involve the successful transport of heavy artillery across a sensitive area. More important still, the secular, left-leaning Jalal Talabani appeared to have come to terms with Iran.[52]

In short order, word issued from Tehran that a reconciliation between the PUK and the KDP had been effected, with their unifying purpose the overthrow of the Saddam Hussein regime. Talabani explained his newfound affinity for the Khomeini regime and the KDP and affirmed that "Iran wants to unify all Iraqi opposition forces because its aim is self-determination for the Iraqi people." Both the PUK and KDP participated in a December 1986 conference in Tehran of Iraqi opposition groups. This setting aside of the differences that had enfeebled the Kurdish opposition for more than a decade appeared to bear fruit early in 1987. With the leadership of the PUK and the cooperation of Iran, an offensive was launched in northern Iraq just weeks after the alarming Iranian attacks at Fish Lake, near Basra. It quickly enlarged the areas under Kurdish control and allegedly provoked governmental retaliation with chemical weapons. The situation had thus deteriorated considerably from the regime's apparent near-compromise with the PUK in 1984.[53]

To offset these negative developments, the Iraqi government made few if any advances in dealing constructively with its Kurdish situation. Saddam Hussein remained dependent on the threat of Turkey's intervention to deter both the Kurds and their Iranian backers. Turkey is interested in the situation with Iraq's Kurds for two fundamental reasons: first, for its repercussions in Turkey's own Kurdish areas and, second, for the security of the vital economic and transport routes that traverse the area, especially Iraq's oil pipeline. The years of Iraq's declining capacity to control its Kurds have coincided with the intensification of Turkey's twin interests. As mentioned earlier, there has been an expanding campaign of violence by the Turkish PKK, which in its first three years claimed more than 600 lives. These operations pose a serious dilemma for Turkey, where political stability depends on a perception of the military's effectiveness and where 8 to 10 million Kurds have been officially relegated to nonstatus as "mountain Turks." Meanwhile, the nearly threefold expansion of the trans-Turkey oil pipeline to a capacity of 1.5 million barrels a day (as of late 1987) has considerably raised Turkey's commercial and economic stake in securing the pipeline against Kurdish attacks.

Through late 1987, Turkey, with Baghdad's permission and blessing, had successfully protected these interests. The Turkish forces' repeated interventions on Iraqi territory entailed direct action against PKK guerrillas.[54] They simultaneously sent strong signals to Iran that Turkey would intervene more deeply still in the event of a Kurdish-Iranian attempt to sever the flow of oil from northern Iraq. Although Iraq's Kurdish dissidents have admitted a desire to avoid an international incident with Turkey by launching an all-out attack on the oil pipeline or the highway, it is far from certain that they will be permanently deterred. Mas'ud Barzani, for example, was quoted in mid-1985 as saying that the pipeline will be sabotaged "when it will have the maximum effect on the Iraqis—when the internal situation deteriorates so much that they cannot cope."[55]

The regime's own actions strongly indicated that by late 1987 the power balance in northern Iraq had shifted noticeably in favor of the Kurds. In the spring and summer of this year, apparently troubled by the increased effectiveness of Kurdish and Kurdish-Iranian operations, the Iraqi military initiated a spring campaign of razing Kurdish villages and relocating their inhabitants to camps in Iraq's western and southern border regions. The precise dimensions of this campaign are not known, but hundreds of villages and tens of thousands of people were believed affected. Reports of this devastation were accompanied by periodic charges that Iraqi government forces used chemical weapons against Kurdish dissident targets in northern Iraq. By most accounts, the regime's campaign has broadened and deepened Kurdish antagonism.[56] The situation, in short, appeared more unstable than at any time in the war – a far cry from the once-promising outlook of 1984.

### Saddam's Leadership

> Yet, were there serious discontent, would there not also be – even under an oppressive regime – rebellion, strikes, flight from the trenches? Would not the seams of a much-quilted social fabric be pulling conspicuously apart?[57]

Passing judgment on the political strength of Saddam Hussein and his regime has become something of an occupational hazard for observers of Iraq during the war. Such political judgments are essential in evaluating all major military conflicts, but they have been given added significance by Iran's sustained demand for Saddam's removal – and for the dissolution of the entire Ba'th Party structure as well – as a precondition for ending the war. At the same time, the shroud of secrecy that has long hindered close political examination of Ba'thi Iraq has been tightened by the pressures of the war. As a result, it is very difficult to obtain a precise idea of the depth or breadth of genuine public support in Iraq for Saddam Hussein and his regime.

These circumstances explain, but only in part, why

most political appraisals of Saddam are tentative in tone and scope. On the one hand, there are analysts who interpret the absence of large-scale disturbances against the regime as "compelling evidence" that the war has not isolated Saddam from the Iraqi people.[58] On the other hand, take the tendency (alluded to at the beginning of this study) to confine political assessments to Saddam's ability to survive whatever military, political, or economic crisis is immediately at hand. Analytical approaches such as these, which can be justified by the objective impossibility of careful political research on Iraq and a media-driven fixation on short-term developments in the war, can be misleading in one important respect. They tend to minimize, if not completely negate, the long-range view and implications of Saddam's ability to survive the war thus far.

In short, ever since Iraq began defending itself against Iranian attacks on its territory in 1982, Saddam Hussein has been viewed as on the brink of political collapse. Five years of constant predictions of his downfall have made it seem that he has escaped by the skin of his teeth from one Iranian offensive after another, from a host of reported coup and assassination attempts, and from the wrath of a population deprived of tens of billions of dollars in benefits from war-wasted oil revenues. By now though, the redundancy of these predictions and the staleness of this image should invite reexamination.

Yet another consideration points to the need to wrench the wartime assessment of Saddam and the Ba'th out of the analytical straightjacket described above—namely, the scope and intensity of the war. By any criterion—its duration, its ideological intensity, the bloodshed involved—the war is an epic conflict. Only one other modern Middle East country—Algeria in its eight-year struggle for independence from France—has persisted so long in a fight for national survival. Something may be gleaned from noting that Iraq's war with Iran is now approaching the length of the Algerian-French confrontation—perhaps that after a long series of contrived "popular revolutions," the Iraqis finally are facing a struggle of genuine national significance and have discovered that they do indeed possess a national will to exist.

Whatever conclusions are drawn about Iraq's political vitality during the war will be difficult, if not impossible, to separate from the personality and capabilities of Saddam Hussein. The most visible trend in Iraqi politics during the course of the war has been the consolidation of Saddam's power and influence. Saddam was well prepared for this development. His decisive influence on the course of political life in Iraq dates to before 1975, well before his formal accession to power as Iraq's president and chairman of the RCC in 1979. In those early years, Saddam cooperated with then-President Ahmad Hasan al-Bakr to prevent military Ba'this from taking control of the regime, as had happened in Syria. Meanwhile, although he deferred to Bakr as the regime's senior statesman, Saddam also moved to "gather the threads of power into his hands."[59] He took a pivotal role in several key undertakings, including the conclusion of the March 1975 Algiers accord with Iran, the expansion of Iraq's role in the Non-Aligned Movement, and convention of the 1978 and 1979 Baghdad summit meetings that drove Egypt out of the Arab League.

In July 1979, Saddam forcibly nudged the ailing Bakr into retirement, taking over the reins of power as the storm of the Iranian revolution was breaking over the Middle East. Shortly thereafter, he ensured his absolute control by physically eliminating over 20 actual or potential political enemies.[60] From the outset, Saddam sought to enhance his personal prestige and acceptability with the people of Iraq. He made numerous informal visits to outlying areas, dispensing gifts and pursuing contacts at all levels and within all segments of Iraqi society.[61]

So on the eve of the war with Iran, Saddam's image consisted of sharply contradictory elements. Because of his bloody ascent to power and his close identification with Iraq's vaunted domestic security services, he was to some the "butcher of Baghdad."[62] Others endeavored to cast him as a pragmatic statesman at the helm of a country whose star was rising in the Middle East and in the Third World.[63] Still others claimed that Saddam's image was shifting "from the remote, ruthless and security-obsessed party hack of the 1970s to the new and popular 'man of the people'" – this by virtue of his attempts at populist appeal and the considerable and widespread benefits resulting from the government's economic policies.[64]

The Iran-Iraq war has magnified, rather than resolved, these contradictions. For one thing, it has sharply inflated Saddam's political persona. From the outset, he branded the war "Saddam's Qadisiyya," a glorifying reference to an epic Arab-Persian struggle from the distant past that by now has forged an indissoluble identity between the war and Saddam. Similarly, there have been massive and coarse embellishments of Saddam's embryonic prewar personality cult. The domestic marketing of Saddam's unifying, father-figure image progressed visibly, yet with confident temperance, during the first two years of the war.

But once the tide in the fighting turned against Iraq, the promotion of the personality cult appeared both to intensify and to lose its poise. Saddam's random visits around the country ceased, but his people relived them in a videotape format. In place of frequent personal and press contacts, impressions of Saddam had to be gleaned from the photographs and posters that peer out from every shop and office and from the larger-than-life figurines that fill the public squares. Finally, great effort was expended on events designed to demonstrate support for the "struggler-leader." Televised parades of young children chanted poetry in his honor; his birthday was established as a national holiday; and the members of the National Assembly signed a compact of loyalty that was written in their own blood.[65]

As clumsy and rigid as they are, such attempts to inundate Iraq's political and popular culture with the image of its energetic leader have by their sheer weight imposed on the public mind the suggestion that there is no true alternative to Saddam's leadership in Iraq. This impression, in turn, has been reinforced in more concrete terms by Saddam's handling of the political crises precipitated by the war. As far as the outside world can tell, Saddam has faced two sharp political challenges during the war, both of which were brought on by significant military setbacks. He addressed both crises in remarkably similar ways and with seemingly remarkable results.

Saddam encountered the stiffest challenge to his authority and power in the spring and summer of 1982. At this time, Iran was climaxing a series of successful counter-offensives that in June resulted in the "voluntary" withdrawal of Iraqi troops from Iranian territory. This humiliating denouement to Iraq's bold 1980 invasion appears to have subjected Saddam to significant criticism from both military and Ba'thi circles. The crisis allegedly came to a head when a group of high-ranking officials demanded that Saddam relinquish his roles of RCC chairman and president of the republic to his predecessor, Ahmad Hasan al-Bakr. The aged and ailing Bakr was apparently the only successor around whom Ba'this could coalesce. Up to this time, Saddam had sought a measure of political authenticity by sustaining an impression of his association with Bakr. Side-by-side photographs of the two men had for three years remained on display publicly and privately. But Bakr's photographs suddenly disappeared in the summer of 1982, indirect evidence that the possibility of reverting to rule under Bakr had been mooted and that Saddam had won out and wanted to underscore Bakr's nonavailability as his potential successor.[66]

But well before this, Saddam seems to have anticipated the pressures that would be brought to bear on him. According to one analysis, he moved early in the spring of 1982 to head off the crisis by conducting "intensive" consultations with his military command structure.[67] Significantly, only after being assured of the military's backing did Saddam move to address matters through the Ba'th Party structures. In late June, apparently at Saddam's insistence, the Ba'th held its ninth regional congress. The secret, four-day affair became the mechanism by which Saddam re-shaped the party's (and the country's) political command to his liking. Seven members of the Ba'th Regional Command (RC) were retired, "possibly for their lukewarm support of his leadership and the conduct of the war," and were re-placed by seven men who had risen through the ranks with Saddam; notably, this adjustment was believed to give the RC a plurality, if not a majority, of Shi'is in its member-ship.[68] Several changes in the cabinet were made, too, but most important of all, the Revolutionary Command Council (RCC) was trimmed from 16 members to 9 and for the first time was made to include Iraq's Kurdish vice president. This radical streamlining and restructuring of Iraq's su-preme leadership conformed to Saddam's ideas of how to govern effectively under crisis conditions. The timing of these changes and the attendant announcements confirmed them to be a scapegoating exercise for Iraq's poor perfor-mance on the battlefield. At the same time, it is significant that, in contrast with past practice, no executions took place; the ousted officials were merely reassigned to ob-scure positions in the party bureaucracy.

The threatening nature of the circumstances in which these political maneuvers took place was corroborated a few days later at Dujayl by an attempt on Saddam's life that is believed to be the closest call he has had during the war. But fewer than two years later, and despite interven-ing reports of further assassination attempts against him, Saddam had regained a good deal of his pre-1982 political stature. Analyses in early 1984 spoke of his "miraculously refurbished image."[69] They declared:

> Mr Saddam is probably more strongly entrenched in power today than he was before he went to war. . . . The president, for all his abuse of power, is seen as the only man strong enough to defend the coun-try. . . . [His personality cult and the secret police] have established him in the popular mind as the only possi-ble leader of Iraq. There is no obvious alternative.[70]

Events pressed on, however, and in two more years the "struggler-leader" encountered yet another political crisis of major proportions. Saddam's predicament in the summer of 1986 followed major military setbacks in the Fao peninsula (in February) and at the central border town of Mehran (May to July), which reduced Iraq to its lowest point militarily since 1982. Within days of the humiliating rout at Mehran, another regional congress (this time an "extraordinary" session) of the Ba'th was called. These meetings were again held in secret, and knowledge of them is limited to the changes they yielded in the high-ranking political bodies of the Ba'th. These changes were much less sweeping than in 1982. Most prominent, one member of the RCC was dropped, Naim Haddad, perhaps the most politically potent Shi'a in Iraq, who had recently retired as the outspoken speaker of the National Assembly.[71] He was soon replaced on the RCC by Sa'adoun Hammadi, the former foreign minister. In addition, three new members—all loyal, hand-picked allies of Saddam—were elected to the RC.[72] Finally, as we shall see a bit later, the accommodation reached at these deliberations apparently included special dispensations for the military, which suggested that Saddam here mirrored the dual political-military approach he used to deal with the 1982 crisis.

These careful and successful manipulations of Ba'thi structures and processes are among the best evidence of Saddam's domination of Iraqi political life. They do not, however, represent fully the range of methods he has used to impose his stamp on the Iraqi polity during the war. There is abundant testimony, for example, that suppression and physical intimidation of citizens for political ends continue to be employed by the regime. Human rights reports issued over the course of the war have endeavored to bring these abuses to light, in the hope that international pressure could persuade Baghdad to discontinue them.[73] Particularly disturbing reports along these lines surfaced in the wake of renewed hostility between the regime and the PUK *Pesh Merga* forces near the city of Sulaimaniya;

they dealt with the government's alleged abduction and torture of children of *Pesh Merga* families.[74] These reports, which are tragic in and of themselves, also play into the hands of those who summarily dismiss Saddam as a narrowly based dictator whose survival depends entirely on brutal suppression of the Iraqi people.[75]

At the same time, however, it should be pointed out that the domestic security services (or *mukhabarat*) have not been given uninhibited free rein over the past seven years. One of the most intriguing political stories in wartime Iraq was Saddam's dismissal of his half-brother, Barzan Ibrahim, as head of Iraqi domestic intelligence and security. Speculation about the reasons for Barzan's removal ranged widely, from an intrafamily dispute over the marriage of Saddam's daughter to the army's outrage over Barzan's heavy-handed interference with the military. A school of thought also developed that suggested Saddam had become sensitive to criticism about the excessive brutality of Barzan and his henchmen.[76] An added indication of the human rights overtones of this strange turn of events came in the State Department's human rights report for 1984, which stated: "The human rights picture [in Iraq] marginally improved in 1984. Arbitrarv arrests and other repressive practices may have diminished somewhat following the removal of the former intelligence services chief in late 1983."[77] The State Department also commended the Iraqi Ba'th Party's effective policies in behalf of the equality of women and the protection of religious minorities, as well as its continuing distance from groups participating in acts of international terrorism.[78]

These accounts do not exhaust the catalogue of Saddam's political strategems. During the course of the war he has issued offers of amnesty to nearly every category of disaffected Iraqis, including military deserters, members of al-Da'wa, Kurdish insurgents, and the ICP. With the exception of the brief dialogue with Jalal Talabani's PUK, however, such gestures have not borne fruit.[79] Saddam has also challenged his political opponents in other interesting ways. In 1983 the regime published a book describing seven plots against his life. Saddam thus boldly dared the Iraqi public to contemplate the possible repercussions of his being removed from the scene, while also conveying an implicit warning to would-be plotters of the strength of his intelligence services.[80] Saddam also erased some of the clannish tint to his regime when, at the same time as Barzan Ibrahim's ouster, he dropped two other half-brothers from positions of authority in the central and provincial governments.[81]

Saddam has also encouraged a limited measure of political institutionalization. In June 1980, Iraq held its first national election since before the 1958 revolution. At that time, a National Assembly was elected to fulfill a decade-old promise made by the Ba'th Party and to seek a more broadly based legitimization of Saddam's relatively new regime, which faced growing pressures from Iran. Although 80 percent of those finally elected to the assembly were active Ba'th Party figures, an effort was made to broaden the candidacy process, for example, by allowing some Iraqi Communists to stand for election. Analysts of this election process argued further that the Ba'thi cadre that dominated the 1980–1984 assembly gave the system a seasoned base of mid-level politicians for the first time since 1958.[82] By the time the second assembly was elected in October 1984, it had become clear that the body had little if any independent authority. Instead, it functioned primarily to express and mobilize support for regime policies. Nevertheless, the assembly does retain some value as an outlet for and barometer of social trends, as shown by the fact that Iraqi women made up a third of the 1984 assembly's membership.[83]

On the whole then, what can be said of lasting significance about Saddam's political performance during the Iran-Iraq war? No simple answers to this question are possible. Yet, the longer the war continues, the more difficult it becomes to accept the minimalist interpretation of Saddam's effectiveness. He has clearly used every tool, method, and resource at his disposal to guarantee his political survival. There is much more to his art than a relentless campaign of brutalization and self-aggrandizement. True, the domestic bloodletting has not ceased even as the war ravages on, and like every other Iraqi government in this century, Saddam's regime has not dared even think of granting broad democratic freedoms to its people.[84] But even Israeli analysts have concluded that Saddam's personality has had a remarkable effect in generating a national sense of patriotism and motivation, though this is acknowledged with almost palpable reluctance: "Lastly, it should not be excluded [from consideration] that Husayn's leadership ability, courage and his determination in adversity had a genuine appeal for Iraqis."[85]

More recent assessments have said much the same thing, drawing similarly positive, but not unqualified, judgments about the success of Saddam's wartime politics:

> To all intents and purposes, it [Saddam's personality cult] has worked: inasmuch as they do not surrender, Iraqis have accepted his leadership and, moreover, have accepted the notion that this was and is a defensive war which Saddam Hussein would gladly end were it not for the intransigence of the regime in Tehran.[86]

> If there is an articulated national consensus, it is that, even if Iraq might have started the war, Iran has pursued the violence beyond all reason. The Iraqis see themselves as the aggrieved party, new peaceseekers holding back a suicidal aggressor who threatens the entire Arab world.[87]

Whatever the degree to which the war has forged an unprecedented expression of cohesive national will in Iraq, it has depended in no small way on the strength and attraction of Saddam Hussein's leadership. Might not this leadership exert a lasting, stabilizing influence on Iraq and lift it out of its condition of perpetual tenuousness into the vitality of a full-fledged nation-state?

## The Potential Transformation of Political-Military Relations

By 1985, the sixth year of its war with Iran, Iraq had become the largest importer of military goods in the world, dwarfing the second-ranking country, Saudi Arabia, by a nearly two-to-one margin.[88] This particular detail merely substantiates what is already well known — as a fighting machine, Iraq's military has experienced an expansion and transformation of its capabilities during the war with Iran. What is less well understood, however, is that Iraq's military may also be undergoing a transformation of its role. The implications of such a transformation could well outlast the war itself.

Iraq has not experienced a successful military coup since 1968. Its last near-successful coup attempt (so far as the outside world knows) was in 1973. Nevertheless, the view prevails among Western observers that Iraq is "a coup-prone country,"[89] evidence of the persistent cynicism with which Western opinion and decision makers have viewed Iraqi politics ever since the bloody demise of the British-backed monarchy in 1958 and the chaotic string of military-led coups in the decade thereafter. Iraq's tradition of a politicized military goes back much further, however, almost to 1921, when the army was established to encourage national unity in the newly formed Iraqi state.[90]

The juxtaposition of this problematic history with the cohesive support Saddam Hussein has received from the military in recent years raises the question of the Iran-Iraq war's long-term effect on the role of the military. After decades of acting primarily as a disruptive force in domestic politics, the Iraqi military has settled, more solidly than many expected, into the role of defending the country against an external threat. Its effectiveness in that role has been criticized repeatedly and justifiably, which does not take away from the political reality that the military has not veered, since 1980, from its commitment to a sustained fight for national survival. And once again it can be argued that the longer and more intense this conflict becomes, the greater the likelihood that it could reverse what had been a first principle of traditional Iraqi politics—the military's inclination to intervene domestically.

The dramatic, war-induced expansion of Iraq's military capabilities is, as Israel and Iraq's Arab neighbors well know, not a new departure in Saddam Hussein's security policy. The urgent development of Iraq's military forces was a Ba'thi policy long before the Gulf war began. "The seven years between 1973 and 1980," according to one analysis, "were the most dynamic in the Iraqi Army's sixty-year history."[91] In this period, for example, Iraq nearly trebled its troop strength, to roughly 250,000 men, without extending the length of military service and despite frequent purges of the military. The rapid acceleration of oil revenues in the 1970s led to purchases of large amounts of more sophisticated equipment for these forces—a great deal was invested in building up the air force, for example. By 1981 Iraq had also diversified beyond Soviet sources of military supply to begin assembly of a comprehensive air-defense system obtained from France and had approached West Germany and Britain as well. Several more divisions of the army were mechanized. All in all, though, these improvements did not appear to buy Iraq a more effective military performance against the Kurdish dissidents, Israel in 1973, and Iran in the opening years of the war.[92]

Great though it was, the rate of military growth in the first 12 years under the Ba'th Party has been far surpassed during the Gulf war. Iraq's total combat manpower strength has risen over threefold, to an estimated 775,000 in 1986. The number of divisions at Iraq's command may now be as high as 40, compared with 20 in 1980. Iraq has registered large gains in major combat equipment, including tanks, armored fighting vehicles, and major artillery

pieces. Significant changes have taken place in the number
and kinds of aircraft and air-defense weapons at the disposal of Iraq's air force. Combat aircraft number as high as
580, nearly double the level in 1980, and a much higher
proportion of these are now top-of-the-line. Combat helicop-
ters have nearly quadrupled, and surface-to-air missile bat-
teries number roughly 75, compared with none in 1980.[93]
An Israeli analyst, taking account of the increased sophis-
tication of Iraq's equipment, its procurement of a strong
defense electronics capability, and the self-corrections
made as a result of combat experience, has concluded that
"the Iraqi army that will come out of the war will be far
superior both quantitatively and qualitatively to the army
that went into it."[94]

From a political perspective, even as the fighting capabilities of Iraq's army began to undergo a transformation in
the 1970s, effective checks on the military's role in domestic politics began to be imposed. There were, for example,
frequent purges of the military, accompanied by a "Ba'thization" of the officer corps; military decision making of any
significance was centralized within the political hierarchy.
Deployment of loyal army units was carefully managed and
strict controls imposed on the air force to defend against a
possible coup, and intelligence and paramilitary services
were set up outside the regular armed forces on a large
scale, again to offset the possibility of antigovernment action by the military.[95]

These steps, and others, were part of a determined,
often brutal, campaign by the Bakr-Hussein leadership of
the Ba'th Party to depoliticize the military in Iraq. Saddam
Hussein played a uniquely important role in undertaking to
stamp out "deviationist" political tendencies in the military.
In the second stage of the July 17–30 Ba'thi coup of 1968, it
was Saddam who personally ushered into exile the non-
Ba'thi military officers who had helped oust the Abdel
Rahman Arif government just two weeks before. He was
keenly aware that previous revolutionary governments,
and in particular the Ba'thi government of 1963, had been

overthrown by military coups. By 1974, most of the Ba'thi
military officers on the RCC had been removed from office.
In the process of taking over the government in 1978 and
1979, Saddam's purges and executions included a large
number of military officers. In the intervening years, according to estimates by Western intelligence officials, military officers were executed or imprisoned each year for allegedly plotting against the government.[96]

Thus, by the time the Iran-Iraq war erupted, a cold but
effective Ba'thi domination of the military was in place that
had prevented any effective challenge to the regime for the
preceding seven years, a clear improvement over the reel-
ing chaos of military coups and coup attempts of the decade 1958–1968. But once the war with Iran began, and
more directly, once it became an outright battle for Iraq's
survival in 1982, the policy of running the military primarily according to the exigencies of domestic Iraqi politics
came increasingly into conflict with the need for maximum
combat effectiveness against Iran. There was clearly a need
for a further evolution in the modus vivendi between the
political leadership and the military, a need that evidence
suggests has not gone unmet.

Analysts of the war have ascribed Iraq's battlefield
failings to many causes — for example, mistakes in military
strategy and tactics. But a good deal of fault has also been
attributed to the suspicion between Iraq's political and military hierarchies and its effect on the management of the
war. The "Ba'thization" of Iraq's officer corps, for example,
one of the prime tools used by the Ba'th Party to keep tight
control of the military, lowered the quality of military pro-
fessionals at the command level. Moreover, the central leadership in Baghdad, and Saddam Hussein himself, have
been directly involved in military decisions at both the strategic and tactical levels. The politically based fear of local
commanders to take any initiative in the absence of direc-
tives from the Ba'thi leadership has repeatedly frozen jun-
ior officers in circumstances requiring immediate tactical
response. Time and time again since 1980 Iraq has reaped

the harvest of its earlier legacy of ensuring that military officers were selected "on the basis of political dedication rather than military competence."[97]

Nor, reportedly, is this the end of difficulties caused by the underlying distrust between the military and political leaderships. Throughout the course of the war rumors have surfaced of attempts by military officers to overthrow Saddam Hussein. Reports of plots and assassination attempts surfaced as early as 1981 and have since appeared with punctual regularity almost every time Iraq's military fortunes have taken a turn for the worse. In each instance, the rumored coup attempt is said to have been discovered and to have resulted in executions of the responsible officers and soldiers. Furthermore, since 1982 there have also been practically incessant stories that commanding officers at various levels of the military have been executed by the regime for poor performance, which includes incurring excessive casualties. On occasion, this practice has been confirmed — by Saddam himself in the case of two generals and one field commander disgraced in the retreat from Iranian territory.[98]

It is impossible to determine precisely the veracity or significance of the alleged executions and coup attempts that have not been confirmed. Even so, it is probably true that some military-based attempts have been made to replace or eliminate Saddam in the past few years and that scores (if not hundreds) of military officers have been executed in an exercise of intimidation by the political leadership. Even if the reports of executions are exaggerated, the chilling effect on the officer corps would be the same. A fully stable equilibrium does not yet exist in the relations between the political and military hierarchies.

At the same time, however, it is not credible to go further and conclude that Saddam's relations with the military are typified by bitter hostility or that they are rigidly locked in a suicidal cycle of distrust and poor battlefield performance followed by scapegoating and more distrust. It is impossible to dismiss lightly the fact that cohesion has prevailed in the Iraqi army through several significant set-backs at the hands of Iran. The following observation, made quite early in the war, remains accurate and probably has greater analytical significance than when it was first made.

> The ground forces have remained united in the face of a war that has been protracted far beyond expectations and despite incessant Iranian propaganda calling for Shi'a revolution in the military. . . . There have been no known incidents of army mutiny or mass desertion, although press reports suggest some officers and men have been arrested for refusing to fight and for conspiring against Saddam. The regime apparently feels confident of the loyalty of much of the population, as is reflected in the widespread military training provided to many elements of the population in recent years and in Baghdad's willingness to dispatch the Republican Guards Brigade to the front several times during the war, leaving the capital relatively unguarded.[99]

Furthermore, beyond these general indications, there have been repeated demonstrations, at key moments, that the regime was willing to compromise in matters of military decision making, which suggests a potentially significant evolution in Iraq's political-military climate. The crisis that attended Iraq's withdrawal from Iran in mid-1982 has already been discussed, with emphasis on the political maneuvers (primarily a Ba'th Party congress and reshuffling of upper-level political figures) Saddam used to reassert his control. During this time, Saddam also made significant approaches to the military. Before the party congress he held protracted talks with his military commanders to ensure their support. Afterward, he went to great lengths in public announcements to ensure that the Iraqi military command was identified with the Ba'th Party decision to pull back from Iran and seek a cease-fire in the war. In the months that followed, other adjustments occurred in the country's political-military balance. A senior military officer was temporarily named to replace Saddam's half-brother as director of Iraq's internal security services. In addition, for a prolonged period, domestic Iraqi reporting on operations at the war front gave visibly greater coverage to the actions of a number of Iraqi corps commanders. Normally the only figure accorded any measure of positive public coverage had been the "struggler-leader," Saddam Hussein. One experienced observer of Iraq interpreted these developments as a clear movement "of senior military officers toward the decision making political center" of the country, an arena that had been exclusively Ba'th domain.[100]

Yet, as succeeding events showed, this development did not solve the problems of Iraq's military performance against Iran nor alter significantly the Ba'thi stranglehold on political process in Iraq. The twin defeats of early 1986, at Fao and Mehran, again showed the inability of Iraqi forces to respond to innovative Iranian tactics, and that high-level political interference remained the bane of the military's existence. Specifically, it was Saddam Hussein who, according to U.S. intelligence sources, was personally responsible for the disastrous decision to leave Iraqi troops exposed at Mehran for weeks.

Again as noted, the political tactics used to contain this crisis were very much reminiscent of 1982 – another Ba'thi regional congress and minor shake-ups in the membership of the RC and RCC. But of much greater significance was a decision by Saddam, apparently made at the July meetings of the Ba'th Party and in simultaneous discussions with the Iraqi general staff, to relinquish an undetermined measure of his control over military decision making to his generals.[101] If the circumstances under which the decision was taken were obscure, its effect was not. Beginning in July, Iraq waged by far its most successful campaign of the war against Iranian economic targets in the Gulf and onshore. The Iraqi air force, which has been criticized for years for a lack of aggressiveness and effectiveness against Iran, made quantum advances in its effectiveness almost overnight. Long-distance raids against makeshift Iranian oil terminals deep in the Gulf and repeated attacks against Kharg Island by low-flying planes using wave tactics reduced Iranian oil exports to fewer than 1 million barrels a day for much of the last quarter of 1986.

These political and military adjustments by Iraq went some distance in neutralizing the Iranian gains made at Fao and Mehran. As is well known, they did not, however, prevent Iran from making a major thrust at Basra in January–February 1987. As this Iranian penetration reached its peak, Iraq delayed for a time before launching a counterattack. U.S. diplomatic sources indicated at the time that a debate was taking place then between Iraq's military and political leadership on whether to counterattack, with the latter expressing great reservations about the casualties that would be incurred. But again, the views of military leaders prevailed, and a counterattack was launched that reclaimed roughly a third of the ground taken by Iran.

This chain of events again demonstrated that Iraq's political and military leaders are flexible enough to communicate and accommodate in the pursuit of national interests. It also shows, of course, that earlier steps in this direction did not conclusively remove high-level political meddling in military decisions. Is there then long-term significance in these shows of flexibility? Given the repeated rumors of military-backed coup attempts and Saddam's past pattern of managing political-military relations, one might well expect him to continue to play cat-and-mouse with his controls on the military. On the other hand, if positive results continue to flow from the regime as it accepts a clear division of labor with the military, Saddam, as a pragmatic decision maker, might be persuaded to accord the military greater latitude in its own realm. Such a development, if it took hold, would alter the equation of mistrust between political and military leaders and clear the way for removal of the most debilitating weaknesses in Iraq's body politic.

## Conclusion

The aim of the above discussion has been to place the war's effect on internal Iraqi politics in a long-term perspective. One problem at the heart of Iraq's perennial political uncertainty has been the absence of a strong national consciousness and of a national will that penetrated the sectarian and ethnic divisions in the country. Over the course of the war, observers have judged with increasing firmness that the sense of national community in Iraq has become stronger. While their commentary has concentrated on the Iraqi Shi'a community, they have also stressed that "a more genuine sense of national identity" and political loyalty have taken shape in the Sunni community.[102] These groups account for the vast majority of the Iraqi population. The Kurdish insurgency, as our earlier discussion showed, clearly does not belong to this national consensus. Concern about this fact has vacillated. At times the Kurds have been badly divided, and for a brief time, it appeared that the regime might make a compact with a major dissident faction. Yet at present, the Kurdish movement is firmly entrenched in opposition to the regime.

Nevertheless, it is probably the Shi'a phenomenon that has overriding long-term significance. While it is too soon to draw unequivocal conclusions, with each passing month the likelihood grows that the Shi'a "triumph of national feelings over religious ones" will prove irreversible. Their "deafening silence"[103] to Iran's revolutionary call gives the Iraqi government a greater measure of assurance about the fundamental loyalty of a larger part of the populace than any regime has ever had. Analysts seem to agree that the influence of the Kurdish insurgency will decline sharply with the close of the war. Khomeini's successor might even eventually cooperate with Iraq to contain the Kurds in both countries.[104] Perhaps more likely is the escalation of Turkish-Iraqi cooperation for the same purpose. Both suggestions point to the strong probability that widespread regional opposition to Kurdish separatism will prevail.

Hence, if the regime resumes negotiations with the Kurds after the war, the prospects of a permanent agreement will almost certainly be better than during the war. In addition, on the Kurds' key demand for greater say over revenues generated by the Kirkuk fields, the Iraqi regime's negotiating latitude might be enhanced significantly as oil production in southern Iraq increases, which would fuel postwar reconstruction and feed the enlarged trans-Saudi pipeline system.

Another problem that has bedeviled Iraqi politics is the concentration of political power in the hands of one man. The war has done nothing to change this. Power lies with Saddam Hussein, now as before. In another sense, however, Saddam's use of that power during the war raises new questions about how and why it remains undiminished and perhaps is stronger than ever. Of course, the domestic security and intelligence services and the Ba'th Party's structure remain central to Saddam's control. But there are also other factors to consider. Batatu's words describing the Ba'th of the mid-to-late 1970s come to mind: "They are also now in closer touch with their people and with reality than at any time since their advent to power. One could even maintain, upon sufficient grounds, that they are more forward-looking than any of their predecessors."[105]

Similar words might apply to current circumstances, if our sources are accurate that Saddam's leadership has been accepted; that his personality cult resonates with Iraqis, so far as they conceive of no other individual with the strength of will to lead the country through the war; and that Iraqis do indeed view the war as a defense against "a suicidal aggressor who threatens the entire Arab world." In this light, Saddam becomes something of an heir to King Faisal I – a contrived father figure for the country who is striving to make the best of a most difficult situation and succeeding well beyond others' expectations.

A frequent theme in the speculation about Saddam's postwar political weakness is the threat he faces from a peacetime army in his "coup-prone" country. There is reason to believe that this threat has been exaggerated. As this study has shown, Saddam has pursued dual policies in dealing with the military. He has enhanced its technical capabilities while purging it of political inclinations. Both policies have stood him in good stead for nearly 15 years. The experience of the war has further redirected the military in Iraq away from domestic political intervention and toward national defense. The intensity of a protracted war against a feared enemy has created a new tradition. The Iraqi military of the future will find that its principal legacy dates from 1980 (the beginning of the Iran-Iraq war) and not 1936 (the first military coup in Iraq). Moreover, that legacy involves a remodeled working relationship with the political leadership, punctuated by the war's numerous and impressively successful instances of flexible cooperation between the military and the political hierarchy. These considerations suggest the possibility that perpetually hostile political-military relations may be more a thing of Iraq's past than its future.

In summary, it must be admitted that our examination of these three variables—national identity, Saddam's leadership, and political-military relations—does not exhaust the scope of valid inquiry into what has taken place in Iraqi politics during the war. Yet it would be difficult to find three factors whose evolution is more central to Iraq's decades-long struggle to achieve national political viability. The mere fact that the conflict with Iran has occasioned, or accelerated, change in these fundamental variables merits serious attention. More to the point, the changes we described appear to have edged Iraq nearer to possible resolution of its endemic political problems. For these reasons, and for others given below in our discussion of Iraq's foreign policies, it would be inexcusable for U.S. policymakers to be as indifferent to post-1980 changes in Iraq as they were to pre-1980 developments.

# 3

# The Emergence of Iraqi
# Foreign Policy

Turkey, Saudi Arabia, Jordan, Kuwait, Egypt—thus reads the list of regional powers on whom Iraq has come to depend for survival. Except for the omission of Israel, it also happens to be the list of the most important friends of the United States in the Middle East. Similarly, the roster of Iraq's bitter enemies—Iran, Syria, and until recently, Libya—incorporates those states that have been America's regional adversaries throughout the 1980s. These parallels suggest, at the very least, a certain congruity between the international outlooks of Baghdad and Washington. Significantly, this coincidence was not generated by the pressures of the Iran-Iraq war. Except for its informal ties with Egypt, Iraq was actually implanted in its present regional alignment well before the war started.

This comparatively long-standing overlap of alliance networks is generally, and incorrectly, overlooked in explanations of why Iraq and the United States resumed full diplomatic relations in 1984. Actually, that resumption was overdue. It could have taken place a good deal sooner, perhaps as the newly appointed President Saddam Hussein forged ties with Jordan and Saudi Arabia, expressed reassurance and support for the existing regional order, and demonstrated "solid evidence . . . of Baghdad's desire to open new economic and diplomatic relations with the West."[1] But narrowing the gap between U.S. and Iraqi worldviews was one thing, and formalizing bilateral relations was quite another. As noted earlier, Washington chose to interpret Iraq's hostility toward Egypt and the Camp David accords as evidence of radicalism, rather than as the turning point in Iraq's emergence "out of a long period of isolation and into the political mainstream of the Arab world."[2] Iraq, for its part, remembered well the alleged U.S. support for the Kurdish rebellion of the early 1970s and had a long history of pique over U.S. neglect of the Palestinians, which Camp David did little to alleviate.

These observations underscore an important theme of Iraq's foreign policy during the war. Baghdad's wartime outreach to a wide range of countries has been an extension of its prewar orientation—pursued more vivaciously and animatedly to be sure, but very much the same principles Saddam set forth before the war. From the perspective of U.S.-Iraqi relations, the major consequence of the war was the shedding of rhetorical contrivances that before had been allowed to stand, but that now impeded a dialogue both parties saw as increasingly important. Restoring diplomatic ties in 1984 was therefore more a formal acknowledgment of the expansion of that dialogue in the preceding three to four years than a bold new departure in policy for either side.[3]

There is a second theme to this discussion. Despite the precedents set in prewar years, the foreign policy Iraq has forged during the war has been surprisingly effective and has contributed greatly to the country's survival. Iraq today has restored trade, military, and diplomatic ties with Egypt, once the "traitorous" cosignor of a peace treaty with Israel. From promising heights of political and economic leadership in the region, Iraq has been forced into a complex web of financial and political dependence on many of its immediate neighbors. Saddam Hussein has publicly recognized Israel's need for a secure existence. Saddam's government has closer relations with the United States than almost any Iraqi regime since 1958 and enjoys its best relations with the Soviet Union since the mid-1970s. Iraq's foreign policy accomplishments, according to its own spokesmen, reflect the maturing of revolutionary leaders once best known for their uncompromising ideological ardor. The purpose of the following discussion is to demonstrate how this maturation process has been accelerated by the war with Iran.

## Cultivating the Superpowers: Lingering Dilemmas

In 1987, after seven years during which the outside world did relatively little to end the war, there was an eruption of diplomatic and military activity designed to curtail the fighting between Iran and Iraq. In response to requests from Kuwait, the United States and the Soviet Union were drawn into parallel roles of protecting Kuwaiti oil traffic against Iranian attacks in the Gulf. The U.S. commitment in the Gulf deepened when the USS *Stark* was mistakenly and tragically hit by two Iraqi missiles in May, which killed 37 U.S. seamen. From this point forward, U.S. naval forces in the Gulf expanded dramatically and were joined by naval patrols from half-a-dozen European nations that signed on ostensibly to protect freedom of navigation in the international waters of the Gulf. This large Western deployment soon overshadowed the Soviet projection of forces in the area and became the target of substantial criticism from Moscow.

Complementing its military undertaking in the Gulf, Washington also vigorously pursued diplomatic measures to develop pressure for an end to the war. These efforts also attracted initial Soviet support and resulted in the unanimous passage of Security Council Resolution 598 in July. This unique resolution ordered Iraq and Iran to cease fighting without having gained prior approval of the demand from the warring parties. Furthermore, as was the case with the projection of naval forces into the Gulf, U.S. and

Soviet diplomatic priorities began to diverge when U.S. officials sought to follow up with sanctions (which were explicitly provided for in Resolution 598) as a way to force Iran to agree to a cease-fire.[4]

Although their ultimate effect on the Iran-Iraq war might prove to be inconclusive, these military and diplomatic initiatives constituted a watershed if only because they amounted to the first serious international effort, with the visible participation of the superpowers, to end the fighting. What was at the root of these dramatic developments? One cause, but essentially a superficial one, was Kuwait's deft diplomatic manipulation of U.S.-Soviet rivalry in asking both superpowers to help protect its tankers. In a deeper sense, however, the developments stemmed from earlier initiatives by Iraq: the "tanker war" in the Gulf that Iraq began in 1984 and Iraq's energetic diplomatic campaign to secure Soviet and U.S. backing for a negotiated end to the war with Iran.[5] Indeed, the highly visible superpower roles of 1987 were in no small way a reflection of Saddam Hussein's careful forging of purposeful relations with both superpowers during the war.

The accomplishment of purposeful relations with the United States and the Soviet Union did not come quickly or painlessly for Iraq. When the war began in 1980, Iraq and the United States had no formal diplomatic relations, though the Carter administration had made periodic attempts to broaden U.S. contact with Baghdad. In 1977, Ambassador Philip Habib stopped over in Baghdad, in response to encouraging signals from Iraqi leaders. Although his meeting with Foreign Minister Sa'adoun Hammadi yielded no breakthrough, it was indicative that Iraqi thinking about the United States had begun to relax. In a personal gesture, Secretary of State Cyrus Vance's physician was sent to Baghdad in 1978 to tend to Saddam Hussein's back problems.[6] In 1979 and 1980, following Iran's seizure of U.S. diplomats at the U.S. embassy in Tehran, there were rumors of attempts by the Carter administration to develop a secret opening with Baghdad, rumors that were fueled by national security adviser Zbigniew Brzezinski's positive public statements about Iraq.[7] But again, no progress in overall bilateral relations could be immediately discerned.

Iraq's relations with the Soviet Union were also under strain in 1980. A 1972 treaty of friendship and alliance provided a broad, positive underpinning to Soviet-Iraqi relations, but gave critics a footing to condemn Iraq's self-proclaimed stance of nonalignment. The heyday of Soviet-Iraqi amity, however, had long since passed. Moscow had bitterly disappointed Baghdad by withholding military supplies during the regime's 1974–1975 civil war against the Kurds. Baghdad in turn disappointed Moscow by failing to consult the Soviets before submitting to Algeria's mediation in its dispute with Iran. Numerous other points of tension included a serious dispute over moving the Soviet embassy from its location very near the presidential palace in Baghdad; the regime's brutal campaign against the ICP; and antagonistic positions on the Ethiopian-Eritrean conflict of 1978, the Yemeni war of 1979, and the Soviet invasion of Afghanistan. The invasion "cooled" Soviet-Iraqi relations "to the freezing point."[8]

Despite the recurrent political tension, military ties between Baghdad and Moscow remained significant. Although Iraq had attempted since the mid-1970s to diversify its sources of armaments, it was still very much dependent on Soviet weaponry when it invaded Iran. But once the fighting began, Moscow instantaneously cut off direct shipments of military supplies to Iraq.[9] Saddam's invasion, using Russian arms, had complicated Soviet efforts to improve relations with Tehran following the demise of the shah. For the first two years of the war, Moscow's clear tilt toward Iran demonstrated the preeminent value it placed on generating an opening with the Khomeini regime. The Soviets threw salt on Iraq's wounds by concluding a treaty of friendship and cooperation with the hated Syrian regime just a month after the war began.

Sources are not unanimous on this, but it is widely

believed that the Soviet embargo on arms for Iraq lasted until 1982. By this time, Moscow apparently determined that a quantum leap forward in ties with Iran was not in the offing. Iran's successful counterattacks had also raised the possibility of an outright Iraqi defeat, which posed a serious challenge to Soviet regional interests. Iraqi officials made clear, however, that the hiatus in arms transfers had not been politically costless. Both the first and second deputy prime ministers of Iraq—Taha Yassin Ramadhan and Tariq Aziz—openly expressed suspicion that the Soviet Union had provided arms to Iran, helping it to expel Iraqi troops. Aziz characterized the Soviets' behavior as "the great mystery of this war." Later, Saddam Hussein also publicly criticized the Soviet-Iraqi friendship treaty for failing to measure up to Iraq's expectations.[10]

The Soviet inclination to improve its standing with Iraq at this time might also have taken into account a relative warming in Iraqi exchanges with Washington. This early phase of progress in U.S.-Iraqi relations was, however, tentative and readily reversible and in no way indicated (as some have suggested) that "the wooing of Iraq [had] become a major priority of U.S. Middle East policy."[11] Rather, things quietly got under way in 1981 when several mild gestures of respect and cooperation were exchanged, which served to break the barriers of mutual unfamiliarity: a middle-ranking State Department official went to Baghdad to discuss Secretary Alexander Haig's "strategic consensus"; the United States joined in a UN condemnation of Israel's attack on the nuclear reactor site in Baghdad; and the size and access of U.S. and Iraqi diplomatic Interests Sections in Baghdad and Washington were expanded. A few eyebrows were also raised when Saddam announced his intent to treat the U.S. representative in Baghdad as if he were a full ambassador, but without according him that status officially.[12]

U.S.-Iraqi diplomacy picked up in 1982. In February, the State Department recognized a shift in Iraqi policies and removed Iraq from a list of countries hit with trade sanctions because of support for international terrorism. Soon thereafter, Saddam Hussein coyly declared that before the war, Iraq's leadership had seriously discussed resuming relations with the United States, but that to do so under stressful war conditions might be interpreted as "begging."[13] Following this, a parade of U.S. visitors passed through Baghdad. Congressman Stephen Solarz, congressional staff delegations, and a member of the National Security Council staff were all granted access to high-ranking Iraqi officials. In these talks, both the United States and the Soviet Union received criticism for failing to exert pressure on Iran to end the war. Finally, in a gesture that suggested that a new fiber of constructive expectation had begun to be woven into bilateral exchanges, Iraq straightforwardly solicited U.S. influence to help bring an end to sales of arms to Iran by Western nations (Israel and others).[14]

With the resumption of Soviet arms deliveries and the proposal for U.S. pressure on Western arms flows to Iran, a basis was laid for the key roles the two superpowers would play in Iraqi policy. In 1983 these roles evolved further when an economic and military crisis forced Iraq's leaders to crank their foreign policy into high gear. One thrust of this policy was clearly to exert pressure on the still-hesitant Soviet Union through multifaceted and rapid-fire approaches to the West. From Washington Iraq obtained $435 million worth of agricultural credits, which supplemented a $1 billion a year U.S.-Iraq trade account that was already three times the level of Soviet-Iraqi commerce. Although they were unsubstantiated and almost certainly false, Moscow no doubt took note of rumors that Iraq was seeking military assistance from the Reagan administration and that Washington was giving Baghdad satellite intelligence to assist in defending against Iranian offensives.[15] In addition, Foreign Minister Tariq Aziz met with Secretary of State George Shultz to urge U.S. support for a UN Security Council resolution calling for an end to the war—one that would include sanctions for noncompliance—

and came away cautiously optimistic that the United States would take action.[16]

But for the United States, Iraq's major attention-getter was its widely publicized acquisition of the anti-ship Exocet missile from France and its attendant threat to strike against Iranian economic targets in the Persian Gulf. Once the Reagan administration realized France was committed to transferring Super Etendard jets and Exocet missiles to Iraq, fear of the war's expansion spurred it into action. The State Department helped initiate a cease-fire resolution that passed the Security Council in October 1983. Iran's rejection of this resolution decisively confirmed a U.S. policy position that Tehran was responsible for the war's continuation. A corollary policy conclusion, made at roughly the same time, stated that the defeat of Iraq would be a major blow to U.S. interests.[17] A State-Defense Department delegation carried this message to Baghdad and its Arab supporters in the Gulf in November. Just weeks later, further support came in the form of presidential envoy Donald Rumsfeld's visit to Baghdad, where he delivered a personal message from President Reagan to Saddam Hussein.

The Soviet Union was similarly uprooted from its passivity regarding the war. Early in 1983, the Khomeini regime cut off the pro-Soviet Tudeh Party's above-ground political activity and expelled a large number of Soviet diplomats. Tudeh members who were not killed or did not escape capture were subjected to show trials that featured televised "confessions" incriminating them as spies for the Soviet Union. This reversal, combined with concern for Iraq's worsening financial, military, and political situation and growing Western influence, rerouted Soviet policy. Arms shipments to Iraq were scaled up sharply, and the number of Soviet military advisers reportedly grew to between 1,500 and 6,000. Saddam for his part ended his boycott of contact with Soviet officials by broaching a dialogue with the Soviet ambassador in Baghdad. The underlying tensions in Soviet-Iraqi relations dissipated quickly at the end of 1983 when a visit to Moscow by Foreign Minister Tariq Aziz touched off an exchange of several high-ranking delegations. Western diplomats in Baghdad, uncertain as to the precise meaning of these developments, nevertheless sensed a breakthrough in Soviet-Iraqi relations was imminent.[18]

The strands in Iraq's policies toward the superpowers came together in 1984, when it achieved lasting breakthroughs with both the Soviet Union and the United States at nearly the same time. Two high-level Soviet delegations went to Baghdad early in the year, and Taha Yassin Ramadhan's trip to Moscow in April confirmed that there was no longer any Soviet hesitation to provide Iraq with maximum levels of military and economic assistance. Iraq was to acquire new weapons systems it had long sought from the Soviets, and military aid across the board flowed more quickly and freely. In addition, a $2 billion Soviet loan, on concessional repayment terms, was given to cover several large economic projects, including oil-field development and a new nuclear power station. Politically, Moscow made a strong but unsuccessful bid to mediate Iraq's feud with Syria, signifying intent to reduce political and economic pressure on Iraq. Public statements by Ramadhan and Saddam gave a high-gloss seal of approval to this overall turn of events.[19]

Baghdad's ties with Washington also began to accelerate at this time. In March 1984, oversight of "Operation Staunch" (the campaign to cut off Western arms flows to Iran) was assigned to Ambassador-at-Large Richard Fairbanks at the State Department to ensure higher level attention in both Washington and foreign capitals. In the same month, mutual restraint and an "agreement to disagree" helped avert a diplomatic falling-out in the wake of U.S. condemnation of Iraq's use of chemical weapons against Iran. Then, at the same moment he was praising the new Soviet attitude on the Gulf war, Saddam also announced that Iraq was receiving assistance from the U.S.-manned AWACS surveillance aircraft that had been sent to Saudi

Arabia when the war began in 1980.[20] Soon afterward, in connection with a UN debate on the recently begun tanker war, Reagan criticized Iran for its attacks on neutral shipping but declared that "Iraq had not gone beyond bounds" in directly attacking its enemy's (Iran's) commerce.[21] Further expression of mutual U.S.-Iraqi interest quickly followed when the Export-Import Bank gave preliminary approval for nearly $500 million in credit guarantees to help build an Iraqi oil pipeline through Jordan.[22] The momentum in these developments pointed unmistakably toward resumption of formal relations between Iraq and the United States. In actuality, Foreign Minister Aziz indicated Iraq's readiness for this step to Secretary of State George Shultz at the UN consultations of late September 1984. Soon thereafter, Saddam Hussein confirmed publicly that the "right time" to reexamine Iraq's severed relationship with the United States would be after the November 1984 U.S. presidential elections.[23] Precisely according to this timetable, the restoration of full diplomatic ties and the exchange of U.S. and Iraqi ambassadors were announced in Washington in late November.

The upshot of these various developments was that by 1985, Baghdad had exploited Iran's intransigence and international isolation to maneuver the superpowers into a common, congenial position on the Gulf war. Secretary Shultz had affirmed earlier that the Soviet Union and the United States had a shared concern about the war—that it not become a hostage to East-West rivalry. Beginning in February 1985, however, discussion of ways to deal with the war and its repercussions became part of an ongoing Soviet-U.S. dialogue on regional conflicts in the Third World.[24] At the same time, both powers have continued to provide Iraq with important support. The Soviet Union's essential contribution has been the full and rapid replacement of any losses in military equipment Iraq suffers in fighting with Iran. Moscow has also upgraded Iraq's armaments when the need has arisen, as indicated recently by Baghdad's acquisition of the highly advanced MiG-29 fighter.[25] For its part, Washington (until the Iran arms scandal) had a quiet, three-pronged approach to assisting Iraq: providing intelligence data on Iran's military, pursuing Operation Staunch, and approving agricultural credits, which in fiscal year 1987 reached a five-year total of nearly $3 billion.

Despite these breakthroughs in Iraq's superpower diplomacy, Iran's surprising military successes in 1986 at Fao and Mehran made it apparent that the risk to Iraq's national survival was far from finished. The concern generated by Iran's superior military performance produced a little-known but potentially important departure in the U.S.-Soviet dialogue on the war. At the U.S.-Soviet regional talks in June 1986, the Reagan administration reportedly proposed a two-part initiative designed to help bring the Iran-Iraq war to a close: first, a joint U.S.-Soviet communiqué opposing the continuation of fighting; and second, a U.S.-Soviet effort to stop arms flows to Iran from both Eastern and Western sources – in essence, an extension of Operation Staunch to include the East bloc. Diplomatic sources indicate that the Soviets' initial response to this proposal was relatively warm – that is, they would consider it; this attitude still prevailed when follow-up contact was made in August. Secretary Shultz at this time indicated that the tone of the U.S.-Soviet regional sessions had improved since 1985 as a result of discussions about the Iran-Iraq war.[26] Nevertheless, in the lead-up to the Reykjavik summit, Moscow declined to give a conclusive response to the U.S. proposal. Only at the UN discussions just before the summit did the U.S. side come to realize, tacitly, that the Soviet Union would not help implement the U.S. plan. This provoked Secretary of State Shultz, in a meeting with Arab foreign ministers, to criticize the Soviet Union for failure to block arms flows to Iran from its friends and allies, as the United States had done.[27]

It is unclear whether secret knowledge of the yet undisclosed U.S. arms sales to Iran caused the Soviet Union to decline Washington's proposal for a joint arms embargo on

Iran. Certainly, sufficient mistrust already existed in U.S.-Soviet relations generally, and sufficient suspicion of competing aspirations for influence in Iran specifically, to make the idea unworkable. Moreover, once the Iran arms scandal became public in November, Moscow had every reason to mistrust the U.S. proposal fully (if only in retrospect), because the State Department had put it forward just scant weeks after National Security Adviser Robert McFarlane's May 1986 trip to Tehran. But significantly, the political and diplomatic maelstrom that the Iran arms scandal precipitated appears not to have included a Soviet denunciation of the U.S. plan of June 1986. The two-part plan described above was quite transparently the model for the U.S. diplomatic campaign pursued at the Security Council beginning in January or February 1987. That campaign had the compound objective of producing a cease-fire and withdrawal resolution on the Gulf war and a companion resolution to enforce an international arms embargo on Iran in the likely event that it failed to heed the cease-fire measure. As noted earlier, the Soviet Union supported the strongly worded cease-fire resolution that was passed unanimously by the Security Council in July 1987. Perhaps predictably, given the history recounted here, the matter of Moscow's support for an arms embargo against Iran proved more problematic.[28]

The July 1987 Security Council resolution coincided with the start-up of U.S. escorts for reflagged Kuwaiti oil tankers in the Gulf. This convergence of events typified well both the strengths and weaknesses of the position Iraq had so carefully cultivated with the superpowers over the course of the Gulf war. First, the events demonstrated that both superpowers retained concern for Iraq's survival in the war. Second, they showed that Iraq had succeeded in maximizing international attention to the dangers of the continuation of the war. Third, however, Iraq's efforts have admittedly produced little that seemed to limit the war. For example, the activist U.S. posture in the Gulf and at the United Nations materialized only after the major embarrassment of the Iran arms scandal, a dear price for Iraq to pay. Discussion of an international arms embargo on Iran was made necessary by the Soviet Union's sustained unwillingness to exert pressure on arms supplies to Iran from its friends and clients—another strong negative for Iraq. Even the UN cease-fire resolution of July was a partial disappointment because its first concrete focus was the tanker war in the Gulf. It thereby encouraged an implicit segmentation of the war, contrary to Iraqi insistence that a cease-fire deal with all fronts of the conflict.

By the time the cease-fire was adopted and reflagging commenced, Washington and Baghdad had experienced a rapid succession of potentially devastating blows to their relationship: the revelation that the United States had sold arms to Iran in open violation of U.S. policies; the expulsion of the U.S. military attaché in Baghdad for taking photographs of convoys of Soviet arms passing through Kuwait;[29] Iraqi charges that Washington had deliberately given inaccurate intelligence data to Iraq, causing the 1986 Iraqi defeat at Fao and the deaths of thousands of Iraqi soldiers;[30] and, of course, the mistaken Iraqi attack on the USS *Stark*. Despite these setbacks, when all was said and done, Iraq and the United States remained harnessed in a working relationship based on mutual, strategically important interests. The willingness to endure damaging, even serious, mishaps and blunders for the sake of these interests suggests that sufficient maturity may exist to support a constructive, long-term U.S.-Iraqi relationship.

### Iraq in the Moderate Arab Bloc

> Iran cannot enter Baghdad because that would mean an all-out Arab war with Iran.
> —Crown Prince Abdullah of
> Saudi Arabia, March 1983

When Iraq restored diplomatic relations with the United States in November 1984, U.S. analysts welcomed the move as an indication that a moderate bloc was developing in the Middle East.[31] The regional focus of their analysis reflected in part a native disinclination to think in terms of bilateral U.S.-Iraqi relations, mainly because there had been no need to do so for nearly 30 years. But there was another reason as well: the fact that the foreign policy of wartime Iraq was acknowledged as a force for moderation in both the significant regional political arenas of the Middle East, that is, the Persian Gulf and the Arab-Israeli zone of conflict.

Its protracted conflict with Iran has confirmed the Gulf to be the primary regional arena of significance for Iraq. To the outside world, the raw volume and content of reporting about the war and the international focus on the tanker war has indelibly identified Iraq with the geostrategic setting in the Gulf. Moreover, Baghdad itself interprets the conflict as prima facie evidence that it has an essential defensive and stabilizing role to play in the Gulf. Indeed, with each passing year of the war and Iran's unchanging refusal to agree to a settlement, the association between Iraq and the Arab states of the Gulf has intensified.

From the beginning of the war, Iraq has been assured of the general, if occasionally quiet, support of the Gulf Arabs. This much was probably guaranteed by their common "Arab-ness" and by the fact that Saddam had assiduously cultivated contact with Gulf leaders after he became president of Iraq. There is also evidence to suggest that some, if not most, of the Gulf Arabs "discreetly welcomed" Iraq's initial attack on Iran.[32] Relatively soon after the war began, a difference in attitude developed between the southern states of the Gulf (particularly Oman and the United Arab Emirates), who face little immediate threat from the Iraqi-Iranian fighting, and the northern states (Kuwait and Saudi Arabia), who are near the cutting edge of the conflict. The southern Gulf countries have tried to keep a low profile on the war, refusing to be drawn into a close identification with Iraq or a direct condemnation of

Iran. The leaders of Kuwait and Saudi Arabia have been more outspoken in their backing of Iraq and, at times, openly very critical of Iran.

But in 1981, while they were providing strong verbal and financial support for Iraq, Saudi Arabia and Kuwait led in organizing the Arab states of the Gulf into the Gulf Cooperation Council (GCC). The formal purposes of the GCC focus on the promotion of economic, technical, administrative, and defense cooperation among its member states. But by omitting Iraq, clearly this subregional mechanism was also intended to institutionalize a certain distance between Iraq and its Gulf Arab neighbors. The rationale for Iraq's omission was probably split evenly between a desire not to alienate Iran, with whom eventual coexistence is universally perceived as inevitable, and lingering fears of Iraqi domination, based on superior size and strength and memories of a radical Iraq's past hostility toward these conservative regimes. Initially, Iraq's leaders expressed sharp disappointment at being shut out of the GCC grouping. They have since spoken well of it, while also hinting broadly that Baghdad would consider an invitation to join if it is proffered at some point in the future.

> Iraq continues to support the Gulf Cooperation Council (GCC) formula of regional cooperation to provide stability and security. Whether the GCC will be the ultimate solution for the region's stability is open to future discussion and consideration, but it will be the model for any future effort.[33]

With these ground rules in place, a rather satisfactory working relationship has developed between Iraq and the GCC states. The GCC and its member states from the southern Gulf have by and large limited themselves to issuing noninflammatory calls for peace and pursuing mediation efforts whenever an opening appeared. But even before the eruption of Iranian-Saudi hostilities at Mecca in July

1987 and Iran's subsequent missile attacks against Kuwait, the GCC issued blunt rebukes of the Khomeini regime on at least two occasions. The first instance occurred after Iran began attacking neutral ships in the Gulf in May 1984. The GCC states pressed the issue at the United Nations and won passage of Security Council resolution 552, which condemned Iran's actions. The second exception was the GCC reaction to Iran's occupation of Iraq's Fao peninsula in February 1986. A hard-hitting communiqué was issued by a meeting of GCC foreign ministers in Riyadh, which condemned Iran's occupation, rejected threats made by Iran against GCC member states, and affirmed its readiness for self-defense.[34] GCC members, including Oman, also criticized Iran's attack before the United Nations.

Beyond heading up most GCC initiatives and several Arab League efforts to wind down the Gulf war, Saudi Arabia and Kuwait have consistently taken the lead in providing Iraq with significant bilateral support. Their help has taken the form of political posturing, financial assistance, and facilitating the shipment of goods (military and otherwise) to Iraq. Estimates of the Gulf states' financial aid to Iraq range widely. One recent estimate, somewhat conservative but well reasoned, puts the amount at roughly $40 billion: $29–31 billion in direct loans and about $9 billion from the sale of Saudi and Kuwaiti oil on Iraq's behalf. This study indicates that the loans were given to Iraq in 1980–1983 and distributed among donors as follows: Saudi Arabia, $20 billion; Kuwait, $6 billion; the United Arab Emirates, $2–4 billion; and Qatar, $1 billion. It adds that Iraq received $9 billion in assistance from counterpart oil sales (which it must eventually reciprocate) in 1983–1985 alone.[35] As for transshipment facilities, Kuwait has consistently answered Iraq's call for such assistance during the war. In 1987, this support attracted international attention because of Iran's accusation that its transport of Iraq-bound armaments made Kuwait a co-belligerent with Iraq, which thereby justified Iranian attacks on Kuwaiti shipping and territory. Iran's campaign against Kuwait clouded the fact that in 1980–1981, Soviet and Eastern bloc shipments coming through Saudi Red Sea ports made Saudi Arabia Iraq's most fruitful arms import channel.[36] Furthermore, beginning in 1986 it was Saudi Arabia that provided a military transportation link of another kind when it apparently allowed Iraqi aircraft to land and refuel after striking at Iranian oil facilities in the far reaches of the Gulf.

Despite this support, Iraq has not always been satisfied with the posture of its Gulf neighbors. In November 1980, just weeks into the fighting, Saddam Hussein remarked that Arab world attitudes on the war fell into three categories: those who completely supported Iraq (Jordan alone), those whose backing was less than complete (the Gulf Arab states), and those who traitorously sided with Iran.[37] Then in early 1983, as Iraqi officials fanned out to approach Western countries and the Soviet Union for military and financial backing, complaints were again made about the insufficient level of Gulf Arab assistance.[38] Although Iraq had by now received roughly $25 billion in direct loans from the GCC states, economic pressures caused by the ever weakening oil market had reduced this aid flow to a virtual trickle. This decline coincided with a major financial crisis in Iraq, caused by the government's insistence on continuing to expend massive sums on economic development.

Iraq's relations with Kuwait have also been subjected to periodic political strains. Early in the war, Iraq petitioned Kuwait for a 99-year lease on two islands that dominate the narrow channel leading to Iraq's only naval base, Umm Qasr. Kuwait refused. It was not as concerned about Iraq's limited access to the Gulf as it was about the legacy of Iraq's 1961 claim over the whole of Kuwaiti territory and the intermittent border clashes of the 1970s. In 1984, Saddam Hussein appeared to scale back the request to a 20-year lease, while implying that Iraq would agree to a final boundary demarcation (a long-standing Kuwaiti wish) in return. Again Kuwait refused. Unconfirmed reports then surfaced in November that Iraqi troops briefly crossed into Kuwait and occupied a strip of contested land, occasioning a secret visit to Baghdad by Kuwait's prime minister and heir-apparent, Sa'ad al-Abdullah al-Sabah.[39] Clearly the threat of Iran has not resolved all the outstanding differences between Iraq and Kuwait.

Significant developments in the meantime, however, suggest that aside from a common fear of Iran, Iraq and Kuwait could be partners in long-term cooperation. The most visible symbol is the two pipelines that bring natural gas from southern Iraq into Kuwait. Kuwait will need the gas for as long as the market-imposed limits on oil production (and associated gas production) continue. But Iraq expects to realize approximately $500 million in annual revenues from the gas pipelines, which it will urgently need as long as the war lasts, and probably well beyond.

There is a similar, perhaps even stronger, argument to make about Iraq's oil pipeline across Saudi Arabia. Saudi Arabia's decision to permit a system of Iraqi oil export facilities to be built on Saudi territory jarred a wide array of cynical assumptions about the longevity and underlying strength of Iraqi relations with the Gulf Arab states.[40] The gesture was fraught with serious implications. It constituted aid to Iraq that was both more tangible and lucrative than previous aid and therefore certainly more provocative to Iran. It raised exponentially the Saudis' risk of being identified by Iran as a co-belligerent with Iraq, while it also provided a target to strike against. From a different perspective, the pipeline has linked the Saudis with a country that historically is far more likely than their own to become militarily involved in a future Arab-Israeli war. Should that occur, the pipeline would provide Israel with a pretext to attack installations on Saudi soil. Finally, the pipeline locks Saudi Arabia into a vital association with a country whose revolutionary, secular outlook has for decades been the antithesis of its own.

Saudi officials, not surprisingly, never stated publicly their rationale for approving the Iraqi pipeline. For the immediate future, they certainly hoped the pipeline would help deter Iran from continuing the war. If not, it would clearly help Iraq sustain itself. In the postwar period, the pipeline would involve Iraq constructively in the life of the Gulf and presumably help dampen any remaining vision Iraq might have of imposing hegemony there. Whatever the reasoning, Saudi Arabia apparently anticipates a long-term relationship with Iraq.

Iraqi foreign policy during the war has also had a significant effect elsewhere in the Middle East, in the broader arena of Arab politics. Perhaps Iraq's most important contribution—certainly its most ironic—has been its deep involvement in Egypt's de facto return to political favor in the Arab community. In a sense, this process began before to the Gulf war, almost as soon as Iraq had finished stage-managing the expulsion of Egypt from the Arab League. Given that perennial realignments among Egypt, Syria, and Iraq are a central feature of inter-Arab politicking, the potential for an Iraqi realignment with Egypt originated with the bitter falling out between Syria and Iraq early in 1979. This Syrian-Iraqi alienation carried over undiminished into the Gulf war, only to be exacerbated when Syria threw its lot with Iran and in the process cut off Iraq's oil export pipeline to the Mediterranean. But the setting became fully ripe for an Iraq-Egypt affiliation when the tide of the Gulf war turned decisively against Iraq in mid-1982, throwing it into a desperate need for a strategic ally to offset (at least in a symbolic political sense) the pressure emanating from Iran. Egypt was the solution.

The outbreak of the Iran-Iraq war proved timely and politically useful for Egypt:

> Coming so soon after the signing of the Camp David Agreements, the war had the multiple effects of distracting attention from the Arab-Israeli issue, of dividing the Arab states which had united to isolate Egypt, and of trapping the orchestrator of that isolation [Iraq] in a desperate struggle for survival.[41]

There was furthermore an element of financial attraction. Egypt had been cut off from Arab economic assistance, and Iraq had been cut off from Soviet military supplies; a coincidence of mutual interests resulted. Even though he had declared the Iran-Iraq war to be a well-deserved pox on both countries, Anwar Sadat approved the sale of some $500 million worth of spare parts and ammunition to Iraq before his assassination in 1981. In 1982, as Iraq retreated from Iran, Egyptian officials expressed serious concern about Iraq's military situation and voiced "a direct interest" in the security of the Gulf. Although they proscribed the use of regular Egyptian troops in the war, some 30,000 Egyptian "volunteers" were estimated to be serving in Iraq's army. And reportedly a number of secret, high-level Iraqi delegations conducted talks on military and political issues in Cairo. By 1983, the accumulated value of Egypt's weapons sales to Iraq was estimated to have reached $2.7 billion, and a new agreement, valued at $2 billion, was reported in 1985.[42]

Under these circumstances, Saddam Hussein began to change the tone of Iraqi discourse about Egypt. The twin thrusts of Saddam's commentary were to stress the differences in behavior and outlook between Sadat and his successor, Husni Mubarak, and to emphasize the organic incompleteness of an Arab world without Egypt.[43] Then late in 1982, in the midst of an aggressive diplomatic campaign directed at several potential allies, Iraq announced that it was prepared to consider the restoration of diplomatic relations with Cairo. Foreign Minister Tariq Aziz, describing Egypt's support as having surpassed "all Iraqi expectations," offered to meet with ranking Egyptian officials to discuss the resumption of ties.[44] But the subsequent dialogue in Paris between Aziz and Egyptian Minister of State Butros-Ghali constituted only a procedural breakthrough, as Iraq made the renewal of formal relations dependent on action by the entire Arab League.

Nevertheless, Iraq's cooperation with Egypt grew closer and sparked similar movement elsewhere in the Arab

world. A major barrier was broken in July 1983. Foreign
Minister Aziz visited Cairo for official talks, which paved
the way for a lengthy list of valuable trade protocols between Baghdad and Cairo. In the following months Egypt's
deputy prime minister was received in Baghdad, and Saddam Hussein issued a call for Egypt's reintegration into the
Arab League.[45] Such gestures by Saddam, who in 1979 had
worked so hard to dismiss Egypt, caught the attention of
other regional leaders. They facilitated Yasir Arafat's December 1983 visit to Cairo and helped catalyze the rein-
statement of Egypt into the Organization of the Islamic
Conference (OIC). Furthermore, Iraq played an important
role in Jordan's active campaign to normalize Egypt's position in the Arab world. This campaign reached a climax in
November 1987 when the Arab League summit in Amman
voted to permit its individual members to resume formal
diplomatic relations with Cairo. Iraq's example in reaching
out to Egypt in previous years and its refusal to condemn
Jordan when it unilaterally restored relations with Egypt
in 1985 were important precursors to the Amman summit.
Finally, Iraq itself resumed ties with Egypt almost immediately after the conclusion of the summit.

Iraq's approach to Egypt during the war indicates that
Iraqi Ba'this have readjusted their once-rigid views of Arab
politics. In perhaps the most dramatic instance of this re-
adjustment, Saddam Hussein has nearly abandoned the
traditional Ba'thi goal of Arab political unity in favor of a
policy that stresses the consolidation and fortification of
the separate Arab states. One can readily trace a Ba'thi
effort to foster a greater sense of Iraqi national identity
back to the early 1970s. At that time, the government's
challenge was to "restructure Iraqi national priorities" by
striking a balance between its ideological commitment to
"pan Arab-dom" and the need for a greater individual loyalty to "Iraqi-dom."[46] As the threat of the Islamic revolution
in Iran began to develop, Saddam's rhetoric seemed to take
matters a step further by declaring that Iraq had to be
strong for the Arab nation to be strong.[47] But even as the

stress of the war has strengthened Shi'a and Sunni loyalties to the Iraqi state, so it seems to have eliminated from Saddam's mind any consideration of broad Arab unity as a practical political goal. Saddam commented in 1982 that

> the Iraqis are now of the opinion that Arab unity can only take place after a clear demarcation of borders between all countries. . . . The question of linking unity to the removal of boundaries is no longer acceptable to present Arab mentality.[48]

Taken in context, Saddam's comments appeared to suggest that "unity" for the Arabs could only be defined in cultural terms, or perhaps by the sense of community among the Arabs that has traditionally formed the basis for solidarity and cooperation. Yet there are other concrete examples of Saddam's pragmatism that would undermine even this limited concept of Arab unity by consensus. Together with King Hussein of Jordan, Saddam at one point responded to Syria's persistent opposition to an Arab summit meeting by proposing that consensus decision making in the Arab League be replaced with decision making by the majority.[49] The underlying message here appears unmistakable: the will of the separate political entities (in this case, Iraq) has gained ascendancy over the elusive will of Arabdom as a whole.

### Iraq and the Arab-Israeli Conflict: Angling toward Accommodation?

> Israel's policy of shipping arms to Iran while treating Iraq as an intractable foe raises serious questions about the judgments being made in Jerusalem. . . . Iraq, [Israel] argues, is a radical Arab state that espouses pan-Arabism, an ideology unyieldingly hostile to Israel. Iran, on the other hand, is Persian, and can be expected in time to revert to its old way of keeping the Arabs at bay while dealing with Israel on matters of common interest. . . .

Israel's policy seems mired in geopolitical thinking of the past. For some time, Iraq has been moving away from Arab radicals toward the Arab status quo powers — Egypt, Jordan, Saudi Arabia. It is too early to tell whether Iraq will follow Egypt's path but the potential for a parallel course is worth noting. . . . The advantage to Israel offered by the possibility that Iraq too will move [toward peace] is too great for Jerusalem to ignore.[50]

This [radical] "conception" of Iraq has helped block out attention, even at higher political levels [in Israel], to the fact that Baghdad has recently been signalling to Jerusalem a change of its stance, possibly even of attitude, not only toward Egypt and the U.S. but Israel as well. . . . Iraq's enmity can no longer be taken for granted as no lesser than Syria's and as far worse than Iran's. The time has come for a reassessment of Israeli policy.[51]

The front-loading of this discussion with the above quotations — the opinion of a current vice president of the American Jewish Committee and an editorial statement from the *Jerusalem Post* — has a twofold purpose. First, it poignantly emphasizes the new day that we are witnessing in Iraq's foreign relations. Second, it is a preemptive gesture, because the argument that Iraq's position toward Israel has "softened considerably,"[52] or is approaching the point of accommodation, is bound to encounter great resistance with many observers and makers of U.S. policy on the Middle East. Nevertheless, as Mr. Moses has written, the possibility is too great to ignore any longer.

As with every Arab country, Iraq's policy toward Israel and the Arab-Israeli conflict is a primary determinant of its relations with the United States. In Iraq's case, this variable probably has even greater significance. One reason for this is the relative paucity of shared interests between Washington and Baghdad, demonstrated by the fact that until the Gulf war came along, both countries seemed content to operate with almost no direct contact. By default

then, Israel and Arab-Israeli issues acquire a dispro-
portionate importance on the still undeveloped bilateral
U.S.-Iraqi agenda. A second reason is the great intensity of
Israel's distaste for Iraq, a sentiment shaped by the consistently polemical Iraqi rejection of Israel's territorial
claims, which goes back to 1948 and earlier.[53]

But along with the other changes he inaugurated, Saddam Hussein seemed disposed to pursue a new tack on this
important issue as well. The two Baghdad summit meetings (November 1978 and March 1979) marked a decisive
end to Iraq's prolonged isolation. Iraq took advantage of
Sadat's compact with Israel to drive for leadership in the
Arab world. This ambition, however, involved Iraq in com-
promises it had previously been unwilling to make. Publication of the November 1978 summit communiqué became
Iraq's first public participation in a declaration that accepted a process of negotiation with Israel: "After studying
the Arab and international situation, the conference asserted the Arab nation's commitment to a just peace based
on the total Israeli withdrawal from the Arab territories
occupied in 1967. . . . "[54] Iraq's public position on the Arab-
Israeli conflict suddenly approximated the land-for-peace
formula enshrined in UN Resolution 242 and implied
that Baghdad "could now accept a Palestinian state on the
West Bank and in Gaza linked to Jordan within a wider
confederation."[55]

Early in the Reagan administration, Iraq fleshed out its
position in unilateral settings. In 1981, in official and private discussions, Iraqi officials affirmed their willingness
to accept a negotiated settlement, if one could be found
that was satisfactory to the Palestinians, and indicated the
necessity of U.S. sponsorship for those negotiations.[56] But
the gesture that seized the attention of even semi-interest-
ed observers was Saddam Hussein's interview with Congressman Stephen Solarz in August 1982. Solarz, an outspoken congressional supporter of Israel, had made his
first visit to Baghdad after several attempts, and just before departing, he met with the Iraqi president. The record

of this conversation reveals an exchange remarkable for both its length and probity. Saddam gave his now widely known dictum that "the existence of a secure state for the Israelis" was necessary to regional peace and added: "There is not a single Arab official who considers in his policy the so-called destruction of Israel and its obliteration from existence."[57] On the Arab-Israeli dispute, Saddam reaffirmed to Solarz that Iraq's decision had been made over a year earlier not to oppose any solution that was accepted by the Palestine Liberation Organization (PLO). A possible West Bank association with Jordan was included, if it was something the Palestinians accepted "without any pressure."[58]

Saddam's remarks went well beyond what any previous Iraqi leader had been willing to have quoted in public. And significantly, it was not until some four months after the interview that a text was published in Baghdad. In the interim, Iraq had gone to the September 1982 Fez summit and again had participated in sponsoring a formulation (the Fahd plan) that provided tacit recognition for Israel in return for a Palestinian state. But when Saddam's declaration to Congressman Solarz was published, the message was direct, unilateral, and unmistakable. Moreover, the timing of publication was provocative. On one hand, it fell in with a broad sweep of approaches Iraq was making to the United States, the Soviet Union, France, and Egypt. On the other hand, it came just after a meeting between King Hussein and President Reagan (who urged the monarch to enter direct negotiations with Israel) and just before the king's tour of Arab capitals for consultations on the Reagan proposal. These circumstances yielded a widespread interpretation that Saddam intended to assure King Hussein he had the latitude he needed to negotiate. *Davar*, the Israeli daily, wrote, for example, that "Iraq's agreement to Jordan's joining the political process will enable King Husayn to feel that his rear is secure."[59]

Both assessments are probably correct. Iraq, at the time of the Solarz interview and its publication, faced an unprecedented national crisis, and Saddam clearly was making a bid for U.S. understanding and support. But from then until 1985 and perhaps 1986, Saddam worked to foster a climate in which King Hussein could maneuver without undue concern for his immediate regional position, first by responding to the Reagan peace initiative of September 1982 and later by conducting his own pattern of diplomacy with the PLO. This meant, for example, that Saddam waited for King Hussein to decline the Reagan initiative before he did so himself.[60] Furthermore, it appears that, contrary to the cynical assessment made by Israel's right wing, Iraq made no serious bid to follow up the Solarz interview by seeking military hardware from the United States.[61]

Other points of reference in this vein of Iraqi policy should receive mention. Tariq Aziz, in Paris only days after publication of the Solarz-Hussein dialogue, reemphasized its major message and underscored its immediate regional application:

> Iraq backed the Fes resolutions because we are not opposed to a peaceful settlement of this problem and hence to negotiations between Israel on the one hand and the PLO and its Arab partners on the other. That is why we are encouraging Mr. Yasir Arafat to coordinate his diplomatic strategy with that of King Husayn.[62]

Aziz was also authorized to respond in a positive, albeit somewhat tentative, manner when he was approached by Secretary of State George Shultz to endorse the U.S.-sponsored troop withdrawal accord between Israel and Lebanon in May 1983.[63] The foreign minister struck another chord, which has become a relatively standard Iraqi response, during his 1984 visit to Washington to restore diplomatic relations. He is reported to have said that Iraq neither opposed nor endorsed the key UN resolutions on the Arab-Israeli conflict—Resolutions 242 and 338—because it is not a direct party to that conflict.[64]

From even a limited historical perspective, the contention that Iraq is not a direct party to the Arab-Israeli conflict is startling. One can scarcely imagine an Iraqi Ba'thi making such a statement, in any forum, just a few short years ago. Now, however, it has become relatively commonplace. Still, it is of a piece with Iraq's prewar loosening of rigid commitments to pan-Arab ideals. Then the trend was incipient; now it is necessarily bolder. One almost senses that Iraq, perceiving itself to be pouring out its human and economic resources in defense of all Arabs, might be on the verge of an Egypt-like calculation—that it "has done enough for the Arab cause and it's time to look out for Iraq."[65]

## Conclusion

The above discussion is but a cursory overview of Iraq's foreign policy during the war. Its focus on political alignments has left relatively untouched the important arena of economic diplomacy, in which Iraq has aggressively met the challenge of maintaining its international financial credibility. A host of creditors, fearful of losing investments already made and guardedly optimistic about a postwar economic boom of immense proportions, have stayed the course with Iraq.[66] In addition, relatively little has been said of Iraq's vital relationships with Turkey and France, either one of which could be represented as a cornerstone of Iraq's genuinely diversified orientation between East and West.

An examination of the maturing of Iraq's foreign policy should also address what Iraq has *not* done—that is, those instances in which Baghdad prudently opted for inaction and silence instead of activism and speaking out. One such instance has already been cited—Iraq's passive response to Jordan's resumption of relations with Egypt, which provoked widespread condemnation elsewhere in the region. The most striking illustration of Iraqi restraint occurred in the wake of the November 1986 revelations of U.S. arms

sales to Iran. After consulting with his diplomatic repre-
sentatives in New York and Washington, Saddam chose not
to exacerbate what was already a very difficult situation
through a confrontation with Washington.[67] He sent a personal letter to President Reagan, and Iraqi officials kept a
tight lid on their direct and undoubtedly blunt exchanges
with U.S. officials, while their management of public pro-
nouncements in Washington and Baghdad clearly reflected
a "damage containment" strategy. Significantly, when the
USS *Stark* incident six months later caught Iraq in a highly embarrassing position, Saddam quickly issued a personal, public apology, agreed to a joint commission to investi-
gate the incident with full cooperation, and confirmed
Iraq's intent to provide compensation for damages to the
ship and losses suffered by the crew. It was a reassuring
diplomatic performance, which helped produce much less
domestic U.S. backlash to the incident than one would have
expected.

But there have also been missteps in Saddam Hussein's
efforts to project an international bearing of respectability
and responsibility. Clearly the issue of chemical warfare has
impeded the rise of Iraq's reputation. It surfaced at a most
inopportune time, early in 1984, just as the tide of world
opinion began to swell against Iran for its rejection of Security Council Resolution 540 and the use of children in its
human wave attacks. The firm consensus internationally
was that despite denials, Iraq had indeed used chemical
weapons against Iran, and thus ended Iraq's free ride with
world opinion. The State Department's March 1984 condemnation formed an essential part of the international
consensus against Iraq. That condemnation, however, was
not a gratuitous or hastily conceived departure. Washington had given at least two warnings of its concern about
the matter,[68] and similar consideration has been tendered as
subsequent U.S. denunciations have been made. Nevertheless, Iraq continues to deny that it is making use of chemical weapons while allegations to the contrary persist. There
can be little doubt that this issue has seriously hindered

Iraq's attempts to eradicate its image as a renegade in international affairs.

Somewhat the same effect resulted when the United States learned that Iraq had provided safe haven for Mohammad Abu al-Abbas, the accused mastermind behind the *Achille Lauro* hijacking. Before this incident, the State Department had praised Iraq for retreating from its earlier support for international terrorism. Moreover, Secretary of State Shultz had assured Congress that Iraq had repeatedly and actively cooperated "against specific terrorist threats to shared interests."[69] Nevertheless, even though Abu Abbas eventually left Baghdad, U.S. concerns about Iraq's ties to international terrorism have not been fully resolved—another disturbing diplomatic loose end.

The purpose of pointing to these problems in Iraq's foreign policy record is neither to detract from nor to minimize the positive metamorphosis that has taken place. In a sense, they are the exceptions that prove the rule. Only by willful and prolonged inattention to the record of the past decade could one argue that these flaws demonstrate Iraq still adheres to an international law of the jungle. Iraq's foreign policy, which has combined Saddam's prewar pragmatism with war-induced necessity, has carefully constructed a wide safety net of political, economic, and military interdependence. It has been no less essential than military tactics or domestic crisis management in ensuring the continued survival of the Iraqi state.

# 4

# The New Iraq:
# Challenges for U.S. Policy

It could indeed be asserted in the nineteenth century
no nation, in the true sense of the word, could be born
without war; that no self-conscious community could
establish itself as a new and independent actor on the
world scene without an armed conflict or the threat of
one.

— Michael Howard[1]

The same goes for twentieth-century Iraq. Its war with
Iran — the most searing challenge the Iraqi nation-state has
ever faced — is the turning point in its modern political development. The Ba'thi regime tried before the war to establish Iraq as a "self-conscious community" and a "new and
independent actor on the world scene," and it achieved some
success. But as Michael Howard predicted, the war with
Iran has intensified this process. Not that Iraq's leaders
preferred this particular means to further their nation-
building purposes: to the contrary, Saddam Hussein declared very early on that Iraq would have been better off
never to have gotten involved in fighting Iran.[2] But it is
involved, and when the conflict does come to an end, Iraq
could well emerge with its internal and international politics
fundamentally reshaped — and for the better.

A striking symbol of the far-reaching changes galvanized by the war is Iraq's growing oil pipeline network. Once Iraq's leaders decided to respond to Iranian and Syrian sundering of most of their oil export routes, they moved aggressively. By the end of 1987, they had acquired the capacity to move 1.5 million barrels a day by pipeline across Turkey and had prepared the way to export 1.6 million barrels a day across Saudi Arabia in 1989. Iraq's burgeoning system of pipelines will prove indispensable to the country's long-term prosperity and security.[3] Despite its tremendous resources, Iraq has never been economically secure because it is nearly landlocked. Since the 1940s, Iraq has been subjected to serious economic and political stress at least once per decade by having its oil export routes severed, and the cutoffs early in the Gulf war were the most damaging ever. But under current plans, Iraq will soon be able to export as much oil as it did before the war, primarily by using export capacities developed since the conflict began and bypassing its prewar strategic outlets in the Gulf and across Syria. This multiplication of its oil outlets has not eliminated Iraq's long-standing vulnerabilities absolutely. But in the long run, the relative reduction of insecurity, achieved through maximum diversification of dependencies, is the most any landlocked country can do. Iraq's war-induced solution to this permanent weakness is already saving it in the standoff with Iran and will continue to reap economic and political dividends for decades to come.

## Challenge One: Assessing a Changed Iraq

From a U.S. perspective, the symbol of the pipeline network helps convey the important message that Iraq is finding its niche. Iraq's leaders are shoring up the country domestically at the same time that they are locking it into a web of accommodating, responsible regional relationships. For U.S. policymakers to become aware of these changes in

Iraq and to assess their significance properly is the first challenge to meet in correcting the persistent blind spot in U.S. policy toward Iraq. What should be recognized is that three long-standing impediments to constructive relations between Iraq and the United States – Iraqi political instability, the hostility of the two countries' foreign policy aims, and Iraq's marginal significance to central U.S. interests in the Middle East – have become obsolete, perhaps for the long term.

To begin with, Iraq's pattern of never quite falling along an axis of major U.S. policy concerns has been broken convincingly. As early as 1983, the situation in the Gulf had developed to the point at which preservation of Iraq's sovereignty and territorial integrity had taken on tremendous regional importance. The United States in turn took the policy position that Iran was responsible for the continuation of the war and that a defeat of Iraq would constitute a major blow to U.S. interests. The heady enthusiasm engendered by this U.S. posture – demonstrated by the Iraqi assertion that the United States now believed "a strong Iraq is an essential prerequisite for peace and stability in the area" – toned down decisively after the Iran arms scandal.[4] But U.S. military and diplomatic activism in 1987 gave the surest demonstration yet that Iraq's continued survival held very high priority among U.S. regional interests.

One can similarly dismiss two other handicaps that have historically held back the development of U.S.-Iraqi relations. The unpredictability or nonviability of Iraq's domestic politics has declined markedly as a deterrent to a constructive U.S. policy toward Iraq. A major portion of this study has been devoted to examining the hypothesis that some fundamental weaknesses in Iraq's political fabric may now be closer to resolution, in part because of the war. If Iraq was not a "real country" when the war began, the war has made it one. Even if policymakers continue to doubt this, U.S. interests for the foreseeable future *need* Iraq to be as "real" a country as possible, which reinforces the wisdom of treating it as one.

On the question of foreign policy, chapter 3 showed that Iraq's international position has changed considerably from the isolated, "rejectionist," and, at times, subversive image it has projected for much of the past 40 years. Saddam Hussein has injected moderation and pragmatism into a wide range of his external policies, from relations with the superpowers and the conservative Arab states of the Gulf to gestures of restraint and acceptance on the Arab-Israeli conflict. This orientation differs sharply from the days when an immediate denunciation was all one could expect from Baghdad in response to nearly any U.S. regional initiative or statement of interest.

But for policy purposes, a full reckoning about Iraq must also attempt to determine whether these changes represent only a temporary, tactical moderation of Baghdad's position, forged of wartime expediency, or whether they are likely to be more permanent. Admittedly, this question will not be resolved with certainty until the war ends and we see how matters proceed in Iraq when it is not under duress. But this does not justify skeptical or necessarily even neutral expectations about the longevity of Iraq's new image, because the war's continuation magnifies the probability that the changes in question will endure. Whatever pressures the war has generated—in schooling Saddam's foreign policies, consolidating Iraq's domestic politics, and elevating its importance to U.S. policy interests—should accumulate, and therefore increase, for as long as the war lasts. Even after major hostilities cease, it is likely that lower (but still significant) levels of Iraqi-Iranian tension will persist. All of this suggests that the influences that have helped put Iraq on the "fast track," in terms of U.S. policy, might continue for some time to come.

There are other reasons to expect that Iraq's new guise will prove to be durable. In discussing the development of both internal politics and foreign policy, the point has been made repeatedly in this study that important changes began to take shape in Iraq well before 1980. In foreign policy, Iraq's prewar metamorphosis included a reduced depen-

during the 1974–1975 civil war with the Kurds and did it again for nearly two years at the outset of the war with Iran. Moreover, when the flow of Soviet arms to Iraq resumed after 1982, there were signs that elements in the Kremlin openly argued against it.[7] Moscow's opposition to follow-up sanctions against Iran, after passage of the Security Council cease-fire resolution in July 1987, also provoked Iraqi chagrin.

These examples delineate how tortuous Iraq's experience in the realm of superpower relations has been. In a little over a decade, the Ba'thi regime has witnessed what it perceived as no fewer than four superpower plots against it. It must be a matter of permanent concern for Baghdad to cultivate ties with both superpowers in a way that minimizes the risk of being cast aside for a larger prize—almost certain to be Iran. The best defense in this regard is to preclude either superpower from taking Iraq for granted by staying on good terms with both, an objective Iraq has skillfully achieved during the past three to four years of the war with Iran. It will have to work even more diligently at it once the conflict ends.

### Challenge Two: Assessing Iraq's Regional Importance and Its Role in the Gulf

The new Iraq presents a steeper challenge to U.S. policymakers than merely assessing the breadth and durability of its political and policy metamorphosis. No, the U.S. blind spot is more pervasive. It also consists of a chronic deficiency in U.S. appreciation for Iraq's importance to the delicate political equilibrium of the region. This deficiency contributed both to the double-dealing Iraq received from the Eisenhower administration as the only Arab member of the pro-Western Baghdad Pact and to the more recent betrayal achieved by the U.S. arms sales to Iran.

Remedying this deficiency requires, among other things, an accurate appreciation of Iraq's inherent strategic weight. Here we can do no more than summarize the high points among Iraq's unique assets. Demographically, it is the largest Arab country east of Egypt. Agriculturally, the Tigris-Euphrates system gives Iraq the capacity for complete self-sufficiency and much more. Militarily, it owns by far the largest and most experienced Arab forces in the Gulf. As for petroleum, Iraq sits atop what are widely believed to be the second largest reserves in the world (after Saudi Arabia), and the bulk of this oil is expected to be recoverable at very low per-barrel costs. Furthermore, if the often-feared stoppage of oil flows from the Gulf ever occurs, Iraq's pipelines (soon to equal Saudi Arabia's in capacity) could become a vital link in preventing the disaster of a complete cutoff of the area's crude to the outside world.

The weight of these variables has not been missed entirely by U.S. strategists. The current secretary of defense, Frank Carlucci, reflecting on a visit to Iraq in 1985, described Iraq as a "pivotal" economic, military, and political power in the region, led by a "thoroughly able and articulate" government cadre. Carlucci's visit took place only a few months after Iraq and the United States restored formal diplomatic relations. Alluding to this, he recalled his feelings in the late 1970s (when he was deputy director of the CIA) that "it was a mistake for us not to have relations, by and large, with Iraq. It is a strategically important country."[8]

How do these strategic assets affect current and future stability in the region? As we have seen, the Iran-Iraq war, and specifically Iraq's capacity to withstand the military, ideological, and cultural onslaught of Khomeini's Iran, has made an issue of Iraq's regional bearing in a manner unseen since the July 1958 revolution in Baghdad. Indeed, an Iraqi defeat by Iran would represent the most serious setback to U.S. interests in the Middle East since the end of World War II. It would therefore seem difficult to minimize either Iraq's regional significance or its importance to U.S. policy concerns. Moreover, given that there is no end in sight to Iran's determination to defeat Iraq and undermine U.S. interests in the Gulf and elsewhere, U.S. policymakers will likely be compelled to acknowledge Iraq's immediate regional importance for yet some time to come.

Still, in the debate about U.S. policy in the Gulf one finds resistance to a positive formulation of Iraq's significance. Its significance is said to be not primary, but secondary; not inherent, but only derived from Khomeini's antagonism to the West and the threat the Gulf war poses to *real* U.S. interests in Saudi Arabia and the unimpeded flow of Gulf oil. Such *de minimis* assessments of Iraq are not conclusive, for they point to other arguments that emphasize the persistent and underlying character of Iraq's regional position. There is, for example, the following provocative historical parallel. The Baghdad coup of 1958, like the possible defeat of Iraq by Iran, involved a threat to the full range of U.S. interests in the Middle East. In 1958, the threat was based on fear that radical Arab nationalism was about to sweep aside all moderate, pro-Western regimes in the region. In the 1980s, the threat has been that an Iraqi defeat would unleash a wave of Khomeini-inspired Islamic fundamentalism and subversion across the Middle East, especially in the Gulf. It should make one pause to realize that Iraq has thus become the decisive proving ground, potentially the turning point, for the two most significant regional ideological movements of the postwar Middle East: Nasser's Arab nationalism and Khomeini's Islamic revivalism. The underlying reasons for this parallel are not clear. But it does enhance the sense of Iraq's regional significance, ideologically and structurally, and reinforces the validity of U.S. support for maintaining the secular status quo there.

Nor is it the case, as some imply, that Iraq's importance depends on continuation of the Gulf war or the presence of the Khomeini regime. The future possibilities, particularly in the post-Khomeini period, are perhaps best seen by showing how drastically conditions in that period will have changed from the assumptions and circumstances of the early 1970s, when the twin pillars policy took hold and excluded a role for Iraq in the Gulf. Salient among the assumptions and circumstances behind that policy were the following:

* Iran was deemed to be the most stable country in the Gulf. The conservative Arab states of the Gulf, in contrast, were in some cases newly formed and of questionable political viability; all of them faced potentially destabilizing social and economic transformations induced by the rapid influx of oil wealth.
* Iran was a conservative state, dedicated to maintaining the regional status quo. This meant, among other things, that Iran acted as a buffer against Soviet influence in the area, was closely aligned with U.S. interests, and was supplied with large amounts of weaponry to police those interests.
* The Arab states of the Gulf, led by second "pillar" Saudi Arabia and encouraged by the United States, acquiesced in this "pax Iranica." Their conservative systems paralleled the constitutional monarchy in Iran, and they felt threatened by the radical and revolutionary program emanating from Iraq.
* Iraq was an anti-Western and anti–status quo force in the Gulf. Its domestic stability was viewed as tenuous at best. It had a new friendship treaty with the Soviet Union and no ties with the United States, and it supported the overthrow of the conservative Arab states of the Gulf.

Although other factors could be mentioned, these should suffice to show that very few of the assumptions underpinning the twin pillars policy hold true now or can be expected to hold true in the future. The conditions that still remain valid are primarily immutable facts of geography: Iran is the largest country and the best situated to block Soviet penetration to the Gulf. But the Iranian revolution convincingly disproved the belief that the shah's was the most stable regime in the area. Nor, after Khomeini's death, will Iran suddenly be healed of its volatility. The question of who will succeed Khomeini as the arbiter of power, as well as the persistence of a host of unresolved political, economic, and social problems, will promise continued turmoil in Iran.

The same can be said of Iran's erstwhile role as a pro-Western, status quo power. The Iran-Iraq war, the consistent hostility the Khomeini government has shown toward the United States and its interests since 1979, its hostility toward the Arab states of the Gulf, its involvement in Lebanon, and its support for international terrorism provide ample evidence that Iran is not now a pro-Western or status quo power. But what of post-Khomeini Iran? At least in part, the U.S. arms sales to Iran grew out of the belief within the Reagan administration that it could forge a strategic opening that would pave the way for Washington to exert some form of influence in a future Iran. But the critical question is, what manner or degree of influence can the United States hope to exert, even after Khomeini's departure?

Realistically, there is an extremely limited scope for U.S. influence in Iran for the foreseeable future. Even if the current intense trend of anti-Americanism dies down, Iranian nationalism, pride, and the memory of years of hostility will prevent any future Iranian regime from embracing Washington in the overweening manner the shah once did. Yet the eventual resumption of just such an embrace appears to have been tacitly expected by the architects of the Iran arms sales: Could anything less have justified jeopardizing the strategic regional balance being contested by Iran and Iraq and the massive deception of our allies in the Gulf and Europe? In other words, there was at the core of the Iran arms sales a regressive impulse to put future U.S. policy in the Gulf back into the same straightjacket that afflicted it in the 1970s, when Washington believed it "had no visible strategic alternative to a close relationship with Iran."[9] What is needed, however, is an alternative strategy for the future that does not involve such heavy dependence on Iran.

Another central factor that has shifted dramatically since the 1970s involves Arab-Iranian relations in the Gulf. The Gulf war and the related tensions between Iran and the Arab states of the Gulf seem to have changed, perhaps permanently, the outlook for a regional consensus on Gulf security. Arab acquiescence to Iranian leadership in regional defense, in the manner of the 1970s, is clearly inconceivable for the present and for as long as Khomeini lives. As one looks further into the future, the outlook remains highly problematic. The submission of the Arab Gulf states to the "pax Iranica" of the 1970s relied on two variables: the close U.S. relations with the shah, which the Arabs believed would keep the shah's regional ambitions in check, and the conservative, status quo orientation that the shah and the Arabs then had in common. As already indicated, future U.S.-Iranian relations are likely to be significantly weaker than in the 1970s, making it unlikely that the United States would soon attempt to persuade the Gulf Arabs to fall in behind Iran again.

Moreover, the nature and intensity of Iran's alienation from the Gulf Arabs, particularly as it was manifested in 1987, could leave a legacy of bitterness and suspicion for a long time to come. Seven or eight years of relative success in keeping the lid on simmering tension between Islamic Iran and the Gulf Arabs came crashing to a halt in 1987. Against Kuwait, Iran attacked ships, was suspected of supporting an accelerated campaign of subversion, and launched repeated Silkworm missile attacks at onshore and offshore installations in the latter part of the year. Equally serious and perhaps of longer term significance were the Iranian-led disturbances Iran in Mecca at the end of July. These disturbances, which resulted in more than a thousand casualties, went to the heart of the Saudi regime's political legitimacy and challenged its guardianship of the holy cities of Mecca and Medina. In turn, Saudi Arabia made the unprecedented gesture of calling for the overthrow of the Khomeini regime and called on all Arab nations to break off relations with Iran.[10] Relations between

Iran and Saudi Arabia were not expected to remain embedded in such hostility, but this bitter incident has made the forging of an Iranian-Saudi consensus in the region a highly dubious prospect.

Iraq's position in the Gulf is the last topic to address in this regional assessment behind U.S. Gulf policy in the 1970s. It hardly bears repeating that Iraq's former hostility to Western and U.S. interests in the Gulf and its subversive posture toward the conservative Arab states of the Gulf are conditions that no longer exist. Moreover, as with the other outdated assumptions of the twin pillars strategy, the change in Iraq's position should not be minimized as a fleeting phenomenon. As shown earlier, Iraq's constructive orientation in the Gulf could well endure into the post-Khomeini era. This assumes, of course, that Iraq survives the war with Iran and that U.S. policymakers do not repeat such mistakes as the Iran arms sales, thereby blindly ignoring the changes that have occurred in the Gulf over the past 10 to 15 years.

## Future U.S. Policy toward Iraq

To begin meeting the challenges and opportunities posed by the "new Iraq," the United States should consider the following policy suggestions. For the near future – say, for the duration of the Iran-Iraq war – U.S. policy must focus on helping Iraq avoid defeat in that conflict. A variety of proposals have been made to strengthen U.S. ties to Iraq during this period. Some have been quite extreme and open-ended, calling for everything short of the dispatch of U.S. troops – advanced weaponry, U.S.-crewed AWACS aircraft for maximum intelligence-gathering capability, and all the economic aid Iraq needs to stay politically and financially solvent.[11] Other less ambitious, more politically realistic proposals are better suited to the twin goals of helping Iraq survive while not gratuitously or permanently alienating Iranian opinion.[12]

Given Congress's responsiveness to Israel's distrust of Iraq, high-profile U.S. military aid to Iraq is unlikely. But if Iran makes major advances in the fighting, there may be sufficient concern to ease some of the political restrictions on U.S. assistance for Iraq. To do so would validate this statement by former Secretary of State Alexander Haig:

> Neutrality [in the Iran-Iraq war] does not mean that we are indifferent to the outcome. . . . We are committed to defending our vital interests in the area. These interests, and the interests of the world, are served by the territorial integrity and political independence of all countries in the Persian Gulf.[13]

Under these conditions, it would become feasible and advisable to provide limited amounts of weaponry to help Iraq accomplish specific (preferably logistical or defensive) military goals. In early 1987, the Reagan administration refused an Iraqi request for C-130 transport aircraft and a proposal by King Hussein to permit Iraq to use Jordan's U.S.-provided counterartillery radar.[14] This is precisely the kind of proposal that should be considered if Iraq's footing worsens substantially. By way of economic assistance, Iraq's access to agricultural credits could be expanded and repayment terms relaxed. In addition, the U.S. Export-Import Bank, which resumed short-term coverage for Iraq in mid-1987, could profitably review Iraq's long-standing request for medium-term credits.

Sustained U.S. diplomatic activism was a key factor in the unanimous UN Security Council cease-fire resolution of July 1987. Iraq had long craved U.S. support of this nature. It also added the soothing touch so sorely needed in the first months after the Iran arms scandal broke. And the Reagan administration exerted consistent pressure in the difficult campaign to gain support for sanctions against Iran for failure to comply with the UN cease-fire resolution. The failure of such sanctions would make it extremely important for Washington to maintain Operation Staunch at a vigorous and visible level, impeding the flow of Western arms to Iran. Finally, if the need arises, Washington could also promote its interests by discreetly encouraging its Arab allies in the Gulf to stay the course in their economic and political support of Iraq.

There is also the postwar period to consider. The United States should take steps to encourage Iraq to maintain its moderate, nonconfrontational stand in regional affairs. To this end, a broader foundation of political understanding needs to be developed between Washington and Baghdad. Unfamiliarity caused by almost 20 years of severed relations remains a problem. A basis for greater understanding has been laid by effective representation at the diplomatic missions in Washington and Baghdad. The mutual Iraqi and U.S. forbearance that sharply limited the diplomatic fallout caused by the Iran arms scandal and the attack on the USS *Stark* provides ample testimony of the rich dividends paid by such representation. In addition, the United States should take advantage of Iraq's strong emphasis on commercial and technological exchange. Expansion of commercial relations would provide Iraq with access to the U.S. technology it has long coveted and U.S. companies with an entrée into the last major unpenetrated Middle East market — probably the most lucrative one in the next 10 to 20 years.

These suggestions embody an objective for U.S. policymakers to pursue with Iraq — namely, the achievement of a consistent and balanced political, commercial, and, if possible, military relationship. The scope of such a relationship would have limits. The difficult history of U.S.-Iraqi relations in the past 30 to 40 years and a number of current strategic and political considerations — including Iraq's continued close ties to the Soviet Union — would almost certainly prevent an intimate or strategic bond from developing between Washington and Baghdad. But these observations should not be construed as minimizing the value of a carefully wrought, limited partnership between Iraq and the United States.

Indeed, this tone of realism is only a reflection of the broader limitations facing the future of U.S. policy throughout the Gulf. As the previous discussion of changes affecting the Gulf since the 1970s suggests, there is a strong possibility that the post-Khomeini Gulf will offer no "pillars" to support an airtight regional policy. The days of the shah are gone and will not return soon, if ever. The fragmentation of power and the hostilities that have afflicted the Gulf for nearly a decade make the best outcome — and probably the first priority of long-term U.S. policy — a balance of power between Iran, Iraq, and Saudi Arabia. In this context, a measured but open U.S. policy toward Iraq is not only realistic but valuable. After 40 years of volatility, realism may yet spawn a sustainable U.S. policy toward Iraq.

# Notes

## Chapter 1

1. Important works to consult include Majid Khadduri's trilogy: *Independent Iraq 1932–1958* (London: Oxford University Press, 1960), *Republican Iraq* (London: Oxford University Press, 1969), and *Socialist Iraq* (Washington, D.C.: Middle East Institute, 1978); Hanna Batatu, *The Old Social Classes and the Revolutionary Movements of Iraq* (Princeton: Princeton University Press, 1978); Edith and E. F. Penrose, *Iraq: International Relations and National Development* (London: Ernest Benn, and Boulder, Colo.: Western Press, 1978); and Phebe Marr, *The Modern History of Iraq* (Boulder, Colo.: Westview Press, and London: Longman, 1985).

2. Abd-ur Razzaq al-Hasani, *Tarikh-ul-Wizarat-il-Iraqiyyah* [The history of the Iraqi cabinets] (Sidon: 1953), 289, as cited in Batatu, *The Old Social Classes*, 25. For discussion of the national identity problem in Iraq, see also Marr, *Modern History of Iraq*, 5–13; Christine Moss Helms, *Iraq: The Eastern Flank of the Arab World* (Washington, D.C.: The Brookings Institution, 1984), 21–36; and Mohammad A. Tarbush, *The Role of the Military in Politics: A Case Study of Iraq to 1941* (London: Kegan Paul International, 1982), 8–30.

3. Phillip J. Baram, *The Department of State in the Middle East: 1919–1945* (Philadelphia: University of Pennsylvania Press, 1978), 174.

4. Memorandum by Adrian B. Colquitt, Division of Near Eastern Affairs, February 4, 1946 (U.S. Department of State, *Foreign Relations of the United States, 1946*, vol. 7 [Washington, D.C.: Government Printing Office, 1972], 568–569).

5. "United States Policy toward Iraq, 1933–1944," Memorandum by the Division of Near Eastern Affairs, Department of State, December 11, 1944 (State Department File 711.90G/12-1144, Record Group 59, Diplomatic Branch, National Archives, Washington, D.C.); and Memorandum from the Office of Near Eastern and African Affairs, July 5, 1945 (State Department File 741.90G/7-545).

6. Telegram from the U.S. Embassy in Baghdad to the Secretary of State, April 17, 1948 (State Department File 501.BB Palestine/4-1748); and Telegram from the Department of State to the U.S. Embassy in Baghdad, April 22, 1948 (*Foreign Relations of the United States, 1948*, vol. 5, part 2, p. 850).

7. Waldemar J. Gallman, *Iraq under General Nuri* (Baltimore, Md.: Johns Hopkins Press, 1964). Gallman was U.S. ambassador in Iraq, 1954–58.

8. Sources for these articles are, respectively: *U.S. News & World Report*, August 25, 1975; *Newsweek*, July 4, 1977; Ihsan Hijazi, *New York Times*, July 2, 1978; *Time*, November 12, 1979; Marvin Howe, *New York Times*, January 7, 1979; Claudia Wright, *Foreign Affairs* (Winter 1979/80); and Adeed I. Dawisha, *Foreign Policy* (Winter 1980/81).

9. Michael Hudson, *Arab Politics: The Search for Legitimacy* (New Haven and London: Yale University Press, 1977), 274–277.

10. Batatu, *The Old Social Classes*, 1133.

11. Some analysts believe that Iraq's isolationist tendencies actually began to wane before 1975. See Edmund Ghareeb, "Iraq in the Gulf," in *Iraq in Transition*, Frederick W. Axelgard, ed. (Boulder, Colo: Westview Press, and London: Mansell Publishing, 1986), 70; Hussein Sirriyeh, *U.S. Policy in the Gulf, 1968–1977* (London: Ithaca Press, 1984), 28–29.

12. See J. M. Abdulghani, *Iraq and Iran: The Years of Crisis* (London, Sydney: Croom Helm, 1984), 157–160.

13. Edmund Ghareeb, "Iraq: Emergent Gulf Power," in Hossein Amirsadeghi, *The Security of the Persian Gulf* (London: Croom Helm, 1981), 219.

14. Ibid.

15. This extraordinary claim was made in the president's address of November 13, 1986 (*Washington Post*, November 14, 1986).

16. John C. Campbell, *Defense of the Middle East*, rev. ed. (New York: Harper & Brothers, 1960), 146.

17. Turkey, Iraq, Great Britain, Pakistan, and Iran made up the membership of the pact.

18. Author's interview with Ambassador Hermann Eilts, November 21, 1986. (Ambassador Eilts headed the political section of the U.S. embassy in Baghdad from 1954 to 1957 and was in charge of Baghdad Pact/CENTO affairs in the State Department from 1957 to 1959.) See also, William J. Burns, *Economic Aid and American Policy toward Egypt, 1955-1981* (Albany: State University of New York Press, 1985), 38, 60-62.

19. Ibid.

## Chapter 2

1. Marr, *Modern History of Iraq*, 211.

2. *Economist*, October 20, 1984, p. 17-18.

3. Ofra Bengio, "Shi'is and Politics in Ba'thi Iraq," *Middle Eastern Studies* 21, no. 1 (January 1985): 2.

4. Ibid., 3-4, 6-7; Hanna Batatu, "Iraq's Underground Shi'a Movements: Characteristics, Causes and Prospects," *Middle East Journal* 35, no. 4 (Autumn 1981): 591; Edward Mortimer, *Faith and Power: The Politics of Islam* (New York: Vintage Books, 1982), 364-365. Of the three, Bengio's analysis is most ambitious, tracing the split in the Ba'th Revolutionary Command Council that brought Saddam to power to the aftermath of the February 1977 riots in Najaf and Karbala.

5. Estimates vary widely of the number of executions carried out by the regime. Batatu ("Iraq's Underground Shi'a Movements," 591), for example, refers to a claim that the regime put to death some 500 Shi'a extremists between 1974 and 1979. Bengio (Shi'is and Politics," 6) cites Da'wa sources in putting the number killed in 1979-1980 at 5,000. The latter figure is believed to be exaggerated.

6. Marr, *Modern History of Iraq*, 237.

7. Chibli Mallat, "Political Islam and the 'Ulama in Iraq," Berkeley, Calif., February 1986, pp. 23-24 (quoted by permission). A revised version of Mallat's paper appears in *The Politics*

*of Islamic Revivalism: Diversity and Unity*, Shireen T. Hunter, ed. (Bloomington, Ind.: Indiana University Press, 1988).

8. Helms, *Iraq*, 31. State Department sources indicate that an estimate of 100,000 to 150,000 deportees gained currency among diplomats in Baghdad at the time.

9. Mallat, "Political Islam," 32–33. It should be noted that these demands might include Iraqi Shi'is expelled during Iraqi-Iranian tensions at the beginning of the 1970s.

10. Bengio, "Shi'is and Politics," 7. The landmark study of the 1980 election is Amazia Baram, "The June 1980 Elections to the National Assembly in Iraq: An Experiment in Controlled Democracy," *Orient* 22, no. 3 (September 1981): 391–412.

11. Saddam's statement in this regard reaffirmed the authoritative formulation on the role of Islam in Arab politics, articulated as early as 1943, by Michel Aflaq, founder of the Arab Ba'th Socialist Party.

12. Mallat, "Political Islam," 30–31; Batatu, "Iraq's Underground Shi'a Movements," 591–592; Bengio, "Shi'is and Politics," 8.

13. Economist Intelligence Unit, "Iraq: A New Market in a Region of Turmoil," Special Report no. 88 (October 1980), 58.

14. Thomas Mullen, "Will Saddam Outlast the Iran-Iraq War?" *Middle East Insight* 3, no. 4 (April–May 1984), 36; and *Economist*, January 29, 1983, p. 46.

15. *New York Times*, September 22, 1987, and *Washington Times*, September 21, 1987.

16. U.S. Department of State, *Country Reports on Human Rights Practices*, vols. for 1983, 1984, 1985, and 1986 (Washington, D.C.: GPO, 1984–1987), the chapter entitled "Iraq" in each volume; "Iraq," in *Middle East Contemporary Survey, 1983–1984*, Haim Shaked and Daniel Dishon, eds. (Boulder, Colo: Westview Press, for the Shiloah Institute, Tel Aviv University, 1986), 483 (hereafter cited as MECS); and Bengio, "Shi'is and Politics," 10–11.

17. Marr, *Modern History of Iraq*, 303.

18. Mallat, "Political Islam," 30–31; Bengio, "Shi'is and Politics," 8–12; and Helms, *Iraq*, 33.

19. Batatu, "Iraq's Underground Shi'a Movements," 583–586.

20. Bengio, "Shi'is and Politics," 1.

21. Mallat, "Political Islam," 7, 28–30.

22. Bengio, "Shi'is and Politics," 12 (emphasis added). Mallat,

"Political Islam," 7, contains an even more parenthetical allusion to "considerations of nationalism" among Iraqi Shi'is.

23. Batatu, "Iraq's Underground Shi'a Movements," 593–594.

24. Helena Cobban, "Coup May Topple Saddam," *New Statesman*, June 26, 1981, p. 11.

25. Barry Rubin, "Holy War in the Gulf," *The New Republic*, August 9, 1982, pp. 10–13. See also, *Washington Post*, August 8, 1982.

26. "Iraqi Shias Pressing Tehran for End of War," Iran Press Service (London), February 3, 1983, p. 1, from Joint Publications Research Service, Near East/South Asia Report no. 2729 (hereafter cited as JPRS), March 30, 1983, pp. 83–84.

27. Jean Gueyras, "Iraq Forges New Unity in the Face of Khomeini's Threat," *Manchester Guardian Weekly*, May 6, 1984, p. 12. See also, from the same time period, *Economist*, March 24, 1984, pp. 31–32; and *Washington Post*, March 20, 1984.

28. Economist Intelligence Unit, *Iraq*, Quarterly Economic Report no. 2 (1986), 11 (hereafter cited as QER).

29. Martin van Bruinessen, "The Kurds between Iran and Iraq," *MERIP Middle East Report*, no. 141 (July–August 1986), 19; Marr, *Modern History of Iraq*, 284–286; Helms, *Iraq*, 30–31.

30. By this time, leadership of the KDP had passed to Mas'ud and Idris Barzani, the sons of Mustafa Barzani. The elder Barzani had died in 1979, in exile in the United States.

31. *Washington Post*, January 7, 1982.

32. van Bruinessen, "The Kurds," 19.

33. Reuter (London), June 6, 1983, as cited in Foreign Broadcast Information Service, Daily Report for Western Europe (hereafter cited as FBIS-WE), June 7, 1983, Annex, 2; *Christian Science Monitor*, July 14, 1983; *Economist*, June 18, 1983, pp. 53–54.

34. *Washington Post*, July 29, 1983.

35. It appears that the PUK's close ties to dissident Iranian Kurds were an important factor in the PUK's subsequent dialogue with the Iraqi regime. Abdul Rahman Qasemlu, head of the major Kurdish dissident group in Iran, reportedly acted as an intermediary in these talks (*Le Monde*, February 9, 1985).

36. *Economist*, January 7, 1984, p. 31.

37. *Times* (London), January 4, 1984; and *Middle East Economic Digest* (hereafter cited as MEED), January 6, 1984, p. 6.

38. *Christian Science Monitor*, May 15, 1984.

39. Ibid.; *Washington Post*, July 29, 1984; see also, *Economist*, September 29, 1984, p. 39; "The Kurdish Problem," Background Brief by the Foreign and Commonwealth Office, London, July 1986.

40. *Washington Post*, July 29, 1984.

41. According to information then current in diplomatic circles, the Barzanis incurred significant problems with local Kurdish inhabitants when Iranian clerics accompanying the thrusts into Iraq insisted on renaming local mountain peaks with Persian and Shi'a Islamic appellations.

42. Phebe Marr, "Iraq: Sociopolitical Developments," in *AEI Foreign Policy and Defense Review*, nos. 3 and 4.

43. Gueyras, "Iraq Forges New Unity."

44. van Bruinessen, "The Kurds," 19.

45. *Times* (London), October 18, 1984; *Washington Post*, October 18, 1984.

46. Voice of Iraqi Revolution in Kurdistan, October 24, 1984, as cited in Foreign Broadcast Information Service, Daily Report for Middle East and Africa (hereafter cited as FBIS-ME), October 26, 1984, E2-4; Agence France Press, June 4, 1985, as cited in FBIS-ME, June 5, 1985; and Colin Legum, *Third World Reports*, London, June 25, 1985.

47. *Al-Sharq al-Awsat*, January 15, 1985, as cited in FBIS-ME, January 16, 1985, E1.

48. *Observer* (London), February 24, 1985.

49. Chris Kutschera, "Inside Kurdistan," *The Middle East*, September 1985, pp. 10–12; *Financial Times*, January 8, 1986.

50. Ibid.

51. *Times* (London), May 20, 1986; *Washington Post*, May 23, 1986.

52. MEED, November 1, 1986, p. 2; *Washington Post*, November 8, 1986; *Economist*, June 13, 1987, p. 44.

53. MEED, November 15, 1986, pp. 20, 23 (quotation); *Economist*, June 13, 1987, p. 44.

54. In addition to the incursions mentioned earlier, Turkey conducted air strikes against targets on the Iraqi frontier in August 1986 and March 1987.

55. Kutschera, "Inside Kurdistan," 11.

56. *Washington Post*, May 13, 1987; *Wall Street Journal*, July 13, 1987; *Washington Times*, September 21, 1987; *New York Times*, September 22, 1987; *Financial Times*, September 29, 1987.

57. Milton Viorst, "Iraq at War," *Foreign Affairs* (Winter 1986/87):360.

58. Ibid.

59. Marr, *Modern History of Iraq*, 215.

60. Marr gives a brief but informative description of Saddam's takeover of the presidency of Iraq (ibid., 229–231).

61. MECS, 1980–81, p. 583; and Helms, *Iraq*, 34.

62. It is no small irony if reports are accurate that this sobriquet originated with Syrian President Hafez Assad, whose own methods of dealing with political opposition leave little to the imagination.

63. Wright, "Iraq – New Power in the Middle East"; Charles Tripp, "Iraq – Ambitions Checked," *Survival* 28, no. 6 (November/December 1986):497; and Arthur Campbell Turner, "Iraq: Pragmatic Radicalism in the Fertile Crescent," *Current History* (January 1982):14–17.

64. Adeed I. Dawisha, "Iraq and the Arab World: The Gulf War and After," *The World Today* 37 (May 1981):188–189.

65. MECS, 1982–83, pp. 565–566.

66. MECS, 1981–82, pp. 587–588; and Helms, *Iraq*, 93–94. Bakr's death in October 1982 probably eliminated the only ready alternative to Saddam's leadership. Moreover, it seems to have cleared the way for Saddam to impose his own stamp on the Ba'th Party's official interpretations of its history and future plans in Iraq (MECS, 1982–83, pp. 561–563).

67. MECS, 1981–82, pp. 587–588.

68. Marr, *Modern History of Iraq*, 303 (quotation); MECS, 1981–82, pp. 590–592. For the proceedings of the congress, see *Ninth Iraqi Ba'th Party Congress Report*, JPRS no. 2738, April 15, 1983.

69. Gueyras, "Iraq Forges New Unity." See also, Marr, *Modern History of Iraq*, 304–305.

70. *Economist*, March 24, 1984, p. 31. A virtually indentical assessment is found in the *International Herald Tribune*, August 6, 1984.

71. Speculation had it that Haddad was removed for criticizing Saddam's conduct of the war. He disappeared after his dismissal from the RCC and was rumored to have been executed. No confirmation of these rumors was forthcoming, and he was subsequently reported to have been seen in Baghdad (QER 1986, no. 4, p. 10).

72. MEED, August 9, 1986, p. 5.

73. See the chapter on Iraq included in U.S. Department of State, *Country Reports on Human Rights Practices, 1980–1986*. See also, the annual *Amnesty International Report* (London: Amnesty International, various years), and two specific AI reports on Iraq: *Iraq: Evidence of Torture* (London: Amnesty International, 1981), and *Reports and Recommendations of an Amnesty International Mission to the Government of the Republic of Iraq: 22–28 January 1983* (London: Amnesty International, 1983).

74. Amnesty International, Urgent Action Release 09/86, "Iraq: 300 Children," January 20, 1986.

75. Committee against Repression and for Democratic Rights in Iraq (CARDRI), *Saddam's Iraq: Revolution or Reaction?* (London: Zed Books, 1986), passim.

76. Helpful summaries of this incident are found in Gueyras, "Iraq Forges New Unity," and MECS, 1983–84, pp. 468–469.

77. U.S. Department of State, *Country Reports on Human Rights Practices*, 1984, p. 1247.

78. Ibid.

79. One of the most comprehensive amnesty offers was issued in February 1985 and was immediately rejected by the Shi'a dissident groups. *Middle East International*, February 22, 1985, pp. 9–10.

80. See a summary of the book in "Seven Plots in 15 Years: Birzan al-Takriti Relates Unknown Event in the 'Assassination Attempts on Saddam Husayn,'" *al-Watan al-Arabi*, June 24–30, 1983, as translated in JPRS L/11520, August 12, 1983, pp. 29–34.

81. The effect of this gesture was mitigated, however, by the fact that Saddam installed other relatives in the positions vacated by these two half-brothers. Similarly, note should be made here of the reported political rehabilitation of Barzan Ibrahim (*Washington Times*, September 3, 1987).

82. Baram, "The June 1980 Elections," 396, 411–412.

83. MEED, October 26, 1984, p. 16.

84. Helms, *Iraq*, 116.

85. MECS, 1982–83, p. 560; see also pp. 564–566.

86. Ralph King, "The Iran-Iraq War: The Political Implications," *Adelphi Papers* 219 (Spring 1987): 11.

87. *Washington Post*, January 25, 1987.

88. U.S. Arms Control and Disarmament Agency, *World*

*Military Expenditures and Arms Transfers 1986* (Washington, D.C.: GPO, 1987), Table 3.

89. *Economist*, October 20, 1984, p. 16.

90. On this early period and the military coups of the 1930s alluded to earlier, see Tarbush, *Role of the Military*.

91. John S. Wagner, "Iraq," in Richard A. Gabriel, ed., *Fighting Armies, Antagonists in the Middle East: A Combat Assessment* (Westport, Conn.: Greenwood Press, 1984), 70.

92. W. Seth Carus, "Defense Planning in Iraq," in Stephanie G. Neuman, ed., *Defense Planning in Less-Industrialized States* Lexington, Mass., and Toronto: Lexington Books, 1984), 37–40.

93. Anthony H. Cordesman, "The Iran-Iraq War: 1984–1986," Eaton Analytical Assessments Center, May 1986, pp. 22–23.

94. Hirsch Goodman, "Iraq: Threat on the Horizon," *Jerusalem Post*, April 5, 1986.

95. A. Abbas, "The Iraqi Armed Forces, Past and Present," in CARDRI, *Saddam's Iraq: Revolution or Reaction?* 215–217.

96. Anthony H. Cordesman, *The Gulf and the Search for Strategic Stability* (Boulder, Colo.: Westview Press, and London: Mansell, 1984), 741, 743; and Carus, "Defense Planning," 36–37.

97. Cordesman, *The Gulf and the Search*, 746 (quotation); Wagner, "Iraq," 78; and Abbas, "Iraqi Armed Forces," 215–217.

98. Helms, *Iraq*, 193. For a relatively complete catalogue of the reports of attempted coups and military executions, see the annual *MECS*, from 1980–81 to the present.

99. Wagner, "Iraq," 79.

100. John Devlin, "Iraqi Military Policy: From Assertiveness to Defense," in Thomas Naff, ed., *Gulf Security and the Iran-Iraq War* (Washington, D.C.: National Defense University Press, 1985), 144–145.

101. *Los Angeles Times*, August 1, 1986; *The Sunday Times* (London), August 17, 1986.

102. Batatu, "Iraq's Underground Shi'a Movements," 593–594; Helms, *Iraq*, 32; Marr, *Modern History of Iraq*, 308–309; King, "Iran-Iraq War," 11.

103. Phebe Marr, "The Gulf War: An Iraqi Perspective," paper prepared for the conference on Regional Implications of the Gulf War, Amman, Jordan, May 1986, p. 21.

104. King, "Iran-Iraq War," 16.

105. Batatu, *The Old Social Classes*, 1133.

# Chapter 3

1. "Iraq: An End to Isolationism," *Time*, November 12, 1979, p. 60. See also, Tripp, "Iraq – Ambitions Checked," 497; "Iraq's New Course," *Newsweek*, July 30, 1979, pp. 49-50; and Abdulghani, *Iraq and Iran*, 157-160.

2. R. D. McLaurin et al., *Foreign Policy Making in the Middle East* (New York: Praeger Publishers, 1982), 2nd ed., 120. See also, Marr, *Modern History of Iraq*, 244, and Dawisha, "Iraq: The West's Opportunity," 151.

3. The expansion of U.S.-Iraqi contacts between 1981 and 1984 is traced in Frederick W. Axelgard, *U.S.-Arab Relations: The Iraq Dimension* (Washington, D.C.: National Council on U.S.-Arab Relations, 1985).

4. *Los Angeles Times*, July 24, 1987; *Financial Times* and *Washington Post*, September 16, 1987; *Baltimore Sun*, September 23, 1987; *New York Times*, November 8, 1987.

5. On the origins of the tanker war, see Frederick W. Axelgard, "The Tanker War in the Gulf," *Middle East Insight* 3, no. 6 (November/December 1984):26-33.

6. These accounts are based on discussions with officials who served in the State Department and White House during the Carter administration.

7. *Wall Street Journal*, February 8, 1980.

8. John K. Cooley, "Conflict within the Iraqi Left," *Problems of Communism* 29, no. 1 (January–February 1980):87-90. Iraq was the first Arab country to condemn the Soviet move into Afghanistan.

9. Iraqi sources claim that Soviet ships carrying 140 tanks to Basra turned around at the Strait of Hormuz and returned home on learning that the war had broken out (Fred Halliday, "Moscow Makes Up to Baghdad," *The Nation*, August 8, 1981, p. 97). The Soviets reportedly fulfilled prior contracts with Iraq to provide small arms and ammunitions and allowed other weapons to be provided through third parties. See, respectively, Dennis Ross, "Soviet Views toward the Gulf War," *Orbis* 28, no. 3 (Fall 1984):438; and Mark Katz, "The USSR and the Iran-Iraq War," *Middle East Insight* 5, no. 1 (January/February 1987):9.

10. *Wall Street Journal*, April 29, 1982; *Washington Post*, November 17, 1982; *New York Times*, November 17, 1982.

11. Halliday, "Moscow Makes Up to Baghdad," 111.

12. Baghdad Domestic Service, June 30, 1981, and INA (Baghdad), July 22, 1981, as cited in FBIS-ME, July 2, 1981, p. E6, and July 23, 1981, p. E15.

13. *Time*, July 19, 1982, p. 46.

14. *Washington Post*, November 21, 1982.

15. *Mideast Markets*, April 4, 1983, p. 12.

16. Reuters, North European Service, May 13, 1983. For a broad discussion of Iraqi foreign policy in this period, see Frederick W. Axelgard, "Out of the Refiner's Fire: The Emergence of Iraqi Foreign Policy," *Journal of International and Area Studies* 1 (1986):49–64.

17. This was the conclusion of an NSC-directed study completed in the fall of 1983 (Richard M. Preece, "United States–Iraqi Relations," Congressional Research Service Report no. 86-142F, July 30, 1986, p. 12, and *New York Times*, January 11, 1984).

18. MECS, 1982-83, pp. 587–588; MECS, 1983-84, pp. 487–488; and author's discussions in Baghdad, December 1983.

19. Ross, "Soviet Views," 440–441; MECS, 1983-84, p. 487; and *al-Majallah* (London), March 31, 1984, as cited in JPRS, May 21, 1984, p. 1.

20. *Financial Times*, May 12, 1984.

21. "Interview of the President," by Martin Bell (BBC) et al., May 31, 1984, Office of the White House Press Secretary.

22. This announcement followed Foreign Minister Tariq Aziz's statement that Iraq considered U.S. willingness to help finance this pipeline as a "crucial test" of good will toward Iraq (*Times* [London], May 5, 1984). This project has not yet begun, however, because Iraq has not received what it deems sufficient political and financial guarantees against a possible Israeli attack on it.

23. *Al-Watan al-Arabi* (Paris), October 12–18, 1986, pp. 30–34, as cited in FBIS-ME, October 12, 1984, Annex p. 2.

24. *Financial Times*, June 9, 1984; *Washington Times*, February 15, 1985.

25. *Washington Post*, March 20, 1987.

26. *Los Angeles Times*, August 9, 1986.

27. *New York Times*, October 2, 1986.

28. See note 4 (chap. 3) above.

29. *Washington Times*, April 20, 1987.

30. *Wall Street Journal*, January 13, 1987; *New York Times*, January 19, 1987; *Washington Post*, January 22, 1987.

31. See articles to this effect in the *Boston Globe*, November 27, 1984, and *Washington Post*, December 2, 1984.

32. Gerd Nonneman, *Iraq, the Gulf States and the War* (London and Atlantic Highlands: Ithaca Press, 1986), 133.

33. Nizar Hamdoon (then ambassador of Iraq to the United States), "Iraq-U.S. Relations," *American-Arab Affairs* 14 (Fall 1985):96.

34. *Middle East Economic Survey* (hereafter cited as MEES), March 10, 1986, p. C4.

35. Nonneman, *Iraq, the Gulf States and the War*, 95–97, 102–104.

36. Ibid., 39.

37. Cited in Tripp, "Iraq – Ambitions Checked," 499.

38. *New York Times*, January 8, 1983.

39. *Washington Post*, December 19, 1984; Nonneman, *Iraq, the Gulf States and the War*, 41–42, 75–76.

40. The contract to complete the second phase of Iraq's 1.5 million barrel a day pipeline to the Red Sea was signed in September 1987, with completion due in mid-1989 (*Financial Times*, September 23, 1987). Iraqi-Saudi discussions of the project date to 1983, and Saudi approval of the pipeline's route across central Saudi Arabia was given in mid-1985.

41. Tripp, "Iraq – Ambitions Checked," 502.

42. *Washington Post*, May 21, 1982; Helms, *Iraq*, 185; King, "Iran-Iraq War," 43.

43. Voice of the Masses (Baghdad), May 25, 1982, as cited in FBIS-ME, May 25, 1982, p. E5.

44. Radio Monte Carlo (Paris), December 28, 1982, as cited in FBIS-ME, December 28, 1982, p. E1; *Washington Post*, December 30, 1982.

45. *Al-Ahram* (Cairo), March 26, 1984, pp. 1, 10, and KUNA (Kuwait), May 3, 1984, as cited in FBIS-ME, March 30, 1984, p. E1, and May 4, 1984, p. E6, respectively.

46. Amazia Baram, "Qawmiyya and Wataniyya in Ba'thi Iraq: The Search for a New Balance," *Middle Eastern Studies* 19, no. 2 (April 1983):188–200.

47. King, "Iran-Iraq War," 15.

48. Voice of the Masses (Baghdad), September 10, 1982, as cited in FBIS-ME, September 14, 1982, p. E5.

49. KUNA (Kuwait), July 31, 1985, as cited in FBIS-ME, July 31, 1985, p. E1.

50. Alfred H. Moses, "Israel Is Placing the Wrong Bet," *New York Times*, March 11, 1987, p. A27.

51. *Jerusalem Post*, August 24, 1987. For other evidence, see "Israel Should Attempt Approaches to Iraq, Say Speakers at Hebrew University Forum," News Release, The Hebrew University of Jerusalem, February 9, 1987; report by Jim Lederman on Israel's reassessment of policy toward Iraq (no title), National Public Radio broadcast of "All Things Considered," October 26, 1987; *New York Times*, November 2, 1987; *London Times*, November 14, 1987.

52. Wolf Blitzer, "Impasse on Road to Peace," *Jerusalem Post* (international ed.), May 9, 1987, p. 10.

53. There seems to be little basis in any history for this negative feeling of a serious Iraqi military threat to Israel's survival; Iraq's involvement in the string of Arab-Israeli wars has been both marginal and ineffective (Wagner, "Iraq," 67–68).

54. As cited in MECS, 1978–79, pp. 262–263.

55. Dawisha, "Iraq: The West's Opportunity," 151.

56. Preece, "United States – Iraqi Relations," 23, citing testimony to Congress given by then-Deputy Assistant Secretary of State Morris Draper, after Draper's meetings with Iraqi officials in Baghdad; Helms, *Iraq*, 11, citing a private interview.

57. INA (Baghdad), January 2, 1983, as cited in FBIS-ME, January 4, 1983, pp. E9, E10.

58. Ibid., E8, E10.

59. Jerusalem Domestic Service, January 4, 1983, as cited in FBIS-ME, January 5, 1983, p. I10. Similar analyses are found in *Middle East International*, January 7, 1983, pp. 6–7; and *Middle East Reporter*, January 8, 1983, pp. 16–17.

60. KUNA (Kuwait), April 27, 1983, as cited in FBIS-ME, April 28, 1983, p. E1.

61. Reference is made here to comments by Israel's then-Foreign Minister Yitzhak Shamir, cited in *Washington Post*, January 5, 1983.

62. *Le Monde*, January 8, 1983, as cited in FBIS-ME, January 11, 1983, p. E4.

63. *New York Times*, May 13, 1983; *Washington Post*, May 16, 1983.

64. MEED, November 30, 1984, p. 18.

65. Moses, "Israel Is Placing the Wrong Bet."

66. Anne-Marie Johnson, "Iraq: Economic Responses to the Gulf War," *The Fletcher Forum* 11, no. 1 (Winter 1987):61–67.

67. Author's discussions with Iraqi officials.

68. See U.S. Department of State, *Country Reports on Human Rights Practices 1983*, pp. 1268–1269 (published in February 1984); "Chemical and Bacteriological (Biological) Weapons," *Note verbale dated 21 February 1984 from the Permanent Representative of the United States of America to the United Nations addressed to the Secretary-General*, 3.

69. *Congressional Record*, June 25, 1985, p. H4918.

## Chapter 4

1. Michael Howard, "War and the Nation-State," *Daedelus* (Fall 1979), 102, as cited in Shahram Chubin and Charles Tripp, *Iran and Iraq: War, Society and Politics 1980–1986*, Occasional Paper no. 1/86, Programme for Strategic and International Security Studies, Graduate Institute of International Studies, Geneva, Switzerland (November 1986), 1.

2. Voice of the Masses (Baghdad), November 4, 1980, FBIS-ME, November 5, 1980, p. E-8 (in a speech by Saddam before Iraq's National Assembly).

3. Besides the ongoing work on the trans-Saudi system, at least two other Iraqi projects have been proposed. A well-studied plan to build a 1-million-barrel-a-day pipeline across Jordan to the Gulf of Aqaba had lain dormant since 1984 because of insufficient political and financial guarantees against an Israeli attack. A third Iraq-Turkey oil pipeline has also been proposed (MEED, September 12, 1987, p. 11).

4. Iraq's First Deputy Prime Minister Taha Yassin Ramadhan ventured this observation (*Middle East Economic Survey*, July 30, 1984).

5. Tripp, "Iraq–Ambitions Checked," 505–506, sums up these questions well.

6. These points were made in a presentation by Geoffrey Kemp, "The Impact of the War on Iraq and the Region," before a symposium on *Iraq and the Bottom Line: U.S. Commercial, Economic, and Strategic Interests in Iraq*, June 18, 1987, Washing-

ton, D.C. Kemp was senior director for the Near East and South Asia on the National Security Council staff from 1981 to 1985.

7. Ross, "Soviet Views," 442–443.

8. Author's interview with Frank Carlucci, then chief executive officer of Sears World Trade, June 4, 1985, Washington, D.C.

9. Gary Sick, *All Fall Down: America's Tragic Encounter with Iran* (New York: Penguin Books edition, 1986), 25–26.

10. *Middle East International*, August 28, 1987.

11. See the *Washington Times* editorial of December 21, 1984.

12. Along these lines, see Daniel Pipes and Laurie Mylroie, "Back Iraq," *New Republic*, April 27, 1987, pp. 14–15.

13. *New York Times*, May 27, 1982. Secretary Haig made this statement in a speech before the Chicago Council on Foreign Relations in May 1982.

14. *New York Times*, April 2, 1987.

# Index

119